GREAT AMERICAN PRESIDENTS

Jimmy CARTER

GREAT
AMERICAN PRESIDENTS

JOHN ADAMS

JOHN QUINCY ADAMS

JIMMY CARTER

THOMAS JEFFERSON

JOHN F. KENNEDY

ABRAHAM LINCOLN

RONALD REAGAN

FRANKLIN DELANO ROOSEVELT

THEODORE ROOSEVELT

HARRY S. TRUMAN

GEORGE WASHINGTON

WOODROW WILSON

GREAT AMERICAN PRESIDENTS

Jimmy CARTER

LOUISE CHIPLEY SLAVICEK

FOREWORD BY
WALTER CRONKITE

Philadelphia

CHELSEA HOUSE PUBLISHERS

VP, NEW PRODUCT DEVELOPMENT Sally Cheney
DIRECTOR OF PRODUCTION Kim Shinners
CREATIVE MANAGER Takeshi Takahashi
MANUFACTURING MANAGER Diann Grasse

STAFF FOR JIMMY CARTER

ASSOCIATE EDITOR Kate Sullivan
PRODUCTION EDITOR Megan Emery
ASSISTANT PHOTO EDITOR Noelle Nardone
SERIES DESIGNER Keith Trego
COVER DESIGNER Keith Trego
LAYOUT 21st Century Publishing and Communications, Inc.

©2004 by Chelsea House Publishers,
a subsidiary of Haights Cross Communications.
All rights reserved. Printed and bound in the United States of America.

A Haights Cross Communications Company

www.chelseahouse.com

First Printing

1 3 5 7 9 8 6 4 2

Library of Congress Cataloging-in-Publication Data

Slavicek, Louise Chipley, 1956-
  Jimmy Carter / by Louise Chipley Slavicek.
    p. cm. -- (Great American presidents)
Summary: A biography of the thirty-ninth president, from his early childhood to his award for the Nobel Peace Prize in 2002. Includes bibliographical references (p.) and index.
  ISBN 0-7910-7646-6 -- ISBN 0-7910-7790-X (pbk.)
 1. Carter, Jimmy, 1924---Juvenile literature. 2. Presidents--United States--Biography--Juvenile literature. [1. Carter, Jimmy, 1924- 2. Presidents. 3. Nobel Prizes--Biography.] I. Title. II. Series.
  E873.S58 2003
  973.926'092--dc22

2003014410

TABLE OF CONTENTS

	FOREWORD: WALTER CRONKITE	6
1	THE NOBEL PEACE PRIZE: OCTOBER 2002	10
2	HOME: 1924–1953	16
3	POLITICS: 1954–1976	32
4	HIGH EXPECTATIONS: 1977–1979	48
5	A CRISIS OF CONFIDENCE: 1979–1981	66
6	CITIZEN OF A TROUBLED WORLD: 1981 AND BEYOND	82
	TIMELINE: THE PRESIDENTS OF THE UNITED STATES	92
	PRESIDENTIAL FACT FILE	94
	PRESIDENT CARTER IN PROFILE	97
	CHRONOLOGY	98
	BIBLIOGRAPHY	100
	FURTHER READING	101
	INDEX	102

Foreword

Walter Cronkite

A candle can defy the darkness. It need not have the power of a great searchlight to be a welcome break from the gloom of night. So it goes in the assessment of leadership. He who lights the candle may not have the skill or imagination to turn the light that flickers for a moment into a perpetual glow, but history will assign credit to the degree it is due.

Some of our great American presidents may have had a single moment that bridged the chasm between the ordinary and the exceptional. Others may have assured their lofty place in our history through the sum total of their accomplishments.

When asked who were our greatest presidents, we cannot fail to open our list with the Founding Fathers who put together this

Foreword

nation and nursed it through the difficult years of its infancy. George Washington, John Adams, Thomas Jefferson, and James Madison took the high principles of the revolution against British tyranny and turned the concept of democracy into a nation that became the beacon of hope to oppressed peoples around the globe.

Almost invariably we add to that list our wartime presidents—Abraham Lincoln, perhaps Woodrow Wilson, and certainly Franklin Delano Roosevelt.

Nonetheless there is a thread of irony that runs through the inclusion of the names of those wartime presidents: In many aspects their leadership was enhanced by the fact that, without objection from the people, they assumed extraordinary powers to pursue victory over the nation's enemies (or, in the case of Lincoln, the Southern states).

The complexities of the democratic procedures by which the United States Constitution deliberately tried to withhold unchecked power from the presidency encumbered the presidents who needed their hands freed of the entangling bureaucracy that is the federal government.

Much of our history is written far after the events themselves took place. History may be amended by a much later generation seeking a precedent to justify an action considered necessary at the latter time. The history, in a sense, becomes what later generations interpret it to be.

President Jefferson in 1803 negotiated the purchase of vast lands in the south and west of North America from the French. The deal became knows as the Louisiana Purchase. A century and a half later, to justify seizing the nation's steel mills that were being shut down by a labor strike, President Truman cited the Louisiana Purchase as a case when the president in a major matter ignored Congress and acted almost solely on his own authority.

The case went to the Supreme Court, which overturned Truman six to three. The chief justice, Fred Vinson, was one of the three justices who supported the president. Many historians, however, agreed with the court's majority, pointing out that Jefferson scarcely acted alone: Members of Congress were in the forefront of the agitation to consummate the Louisiana Purchase and Congress voted to fund it.

With more than two centuries of history and precedent now behind us, the Constitution is still found to be flexible when honest and sincere individuals support their own causes with quite different readings of it. These are the questions that end up for interpretation by the Supreme Court.

As late as the early years of the twenty-first century, perhaps the most fateful decision any president ever can make—to commit the nation to war—was again debated and precedent ignored. The Constitution says that only the Congress has the authority to declare war. Yet the Congress, with the objection of few members, ignored this Constitutional provision and voted to give President George W. Bush the right to take the United States to war whenever and under whatever conditions he decided.

Thus a president's place in history may well be determined by how much power he seizes or is granted in

Foreword

re-interpreting and circumventing the remarkable document that is the Constitution. Although the Founding Fathers thought they had spelled out the president's authority in their clear division of powers between the branches of the executive, the legislative and the judiciary, their wisdom has been challenged frequently by ensuing generations. The need and the demand for change is dictated by the march of events, the vast alterations in society, the global condition beyond our influence, and the progress of technology far beyond the imaginations of any of the generations which preceded them.

The extent to which the powers of the presidency will be enhanced and utilized by the chief executives to come in large degree will depend, as they have throughout our history, on the character of the presidents themselves. The limitations on those powers, in turn, will depend on the strength and will of those other two legs of the three-legged stool of American government—the legislative and the judiciary.

And as long as this nation remains a democracy, the final say will rest with an educated electorate in perpetual exercise of its constitutional rights to free speech and a free and alert press.

1

THE NOBEL PEACE PRIZE:
OCTOBER 2002

AT APPROXIMATELY 4:00 A.M. on October 11, 2002, former president Jimmy Carter was awakened at his home in Plains, Georgia, by the sound of a ringing telephone. The call was from a representative of the Nobel Committee in Oslo, Norway, and the news was thrilling. The 78-year-old Carter had just been notified that he had won the prestigious Nobel Peace Prize. Only two other U.S. presidents had achieved this honor—Theodore Roosevelt in 1906 and Woodrow Wilson in 1919.

Carter was awarded the Peace Prize in part for actions he had taken during his term in office (1977–1981). As president, the Nobel citation declared, "Carter's mediation was a vital

THE NOBEL PEACE PRIZE: OCTOBER 2002

Jimmy Carter was awarded the 2002 Nobel Peace Prize for his work toward peace during his term as president and after he left office. He was the third president to win the Peace Prize, after Theodore Roosevelt and Woodrow Wilson, who won in 1906 and 1919, respectively. He accepted the prize in Oslo City Hall in Norway on December 10, 2002.

contribution to the Camp David Accords," the framework for a peace agreement between Israel and Egypt. The two countries had been steadfast enemies for more than three decades. Carter was also hailed for putting new "emphasis on the place of human rights in international politics" during his four years in the White House.

But it was, above all, Carter's remarkable activities as a private citizen that had convinced the Nobel Committee to choose him from among a field of more than 150 nominees for the Peace Prize. In 1982, the former president and his wife Rosalynn had established the Carter Center. Located in Atlanta, Georgia, the center is a public policy institute designed to continue the work Carter had begun while in office. As noted in the Nobel Committee's citation, this undertaking showed his commitment to advancing international peace and human rights and to promoting social and economic development in impoverished countries around the globe. Since the center's founding, Carter has served as an observer of political elections in numerous developing democracies. He has participated in conflict resolution in trouble spots from Haiti to Venezuela and has helped provide health care, shelter, and training in modern agricultural techniques to the poor on several continents.

Never before in the history of the United States had there been an ex-president like Jimmy Carter. Although a handful of other chief executives, particularly John Quincy Adams, William Howard Taft, and Herbert Hoover, remained actively involved in public service after leaving the White House, Carter's post-presidential contributions as an international peacemaker, humanitarian, and tireless champion of human rights is unique.

Not surprisingly, Carter's post-presidential career has gained him the affection and admiration of millions in his own country and around the world. Yet despite the

Excerpts from the Nobel Peace Prize Announcement of October 11, 2002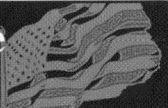

The Norwegian Nobel Committee has decided to award the Nobel Peace Prize for 2002 to Jimmy Carter, for his decades of untiring effort to find peaceful solutions to international conflicts, to advance democracy and human rights, and to promote economic and social development.

During his presidency (1977–1981), Carter's mediation was a vital contribution to the Camp David Accords between Israel and Egypt, in itself a great enough achievement to qualify for the Nobel Peace Prize. . . .

Through his Carter Center . . . Carter has since his presidency undertaken very extensive and persevering conflict resolution on several continents.

He has shown outstanding commitment to human rights, and has served as an observer at countless elections all over the world.

He has worked hard on many fronts to fight tropical diseases and to bring about growth and progress in developing countries. . . .

In a situation currently marked by threats of the use of power, Carter has stood by the principles that conflicts must as far as possible be resolved through mediation and international cooperation based on international law, respect for human rights, and economic development.

Jimmy Carter

Carter and his wife Rosalynn observe an election in Nigeria. The Carters founded the Carter Center in Atlanta in 1982 for the purpose of advancing international peace and human rights, partly through ensuring and observing democratic elections in developing and impoverished nations, such as this one in Nigeria.

widespread respect he enjoys today, Carter was frequently and harshly criticized during his presidency. He grappled with a host of pressing challenges, from the Soviet invasion of Afghanistan and the Iranian hostage crisis abroad to an economic crisis at home. Although most Americans believed Carter to be an honest and decent man, rising energy costs and inflation that raised the price of goods without increasing their value made many conclude he was an ineffectual leader.

The Nobel Peace Prize: October 2002

Now, with the benefit of historical perspective, Carter's presidency is being viewed in a more sympathetic light. A quarter century after the one-term Georgia governor rose from almost complete anonymity to claim the Democratic nomination and then the presidency in 1976, many scholars are finally beginning to pay more attention to Carter's accomplishments in the White House than to his failures. No one can foretell where Jimmy Carter's presidency ultimately will be ranked in U.S. history, but it appears certain that his reputation as one of America's most public-spirited and influential ex-presidents will stand the test of time.

2

HOME: 1924–1953

JAMES EARL CARTER, JR., was born on October 1, 1924, in the tiny town of Plains in southwestern Georgia. Four years later, Jimmy (as he was nicknamed from the start), his parents, and his younger sister Gloria moved to a farm in the even smaller community of Archery, about three miles west of Plains.

"THE MOST SUCCESSFUL MAN HERE"
Jimmy's father, Earl Carter, was ambitious and hardworking. By the time he was in his mid-twenties, he owned a general store, icehouse, and laundry in Plains. Earl, however, wanted more. Believing that land ownership was the surest path to wealth and

Home: 1924–1953

James Earl Carter, Jr., pictured here with his younger sister Gloria, was born on October 1, 1924, in Plains, Georgia. Four years later, his family moved to Archery, a smaller town a few miles from Plains. Earl Carter, Jimmy's father, was a successful farmer and storeowner, but he was careful with money, so the Carter family did not live in luxury.

prestige in his rural society, he began buying up tracts of farmland outside of Plains. Earl's relentless drive to get ahead made him stand out in his little hometown. In 1923, at the age of 29, he married Lillian Gordy. Lillian, a nurse, had started dating him a year earlier, after the doctor she worked for advised her that Earl Carter "is going to be the most successful man here."

After the Carters moved to Archery, Earl channeled his considerable energy into building up his new 350-acre farm. He grew peanuts, cotton, sugarcane, sweet potatoes, and watermelon. The crops were planted, cultivated, and harvested at a very low cost to him, because most of the work was done for low wages by the impoverished black men and women who lived in Archery. Eventually, Earl would hire upwards of 200 African Americans to labor in his fields at harvest time.

Five African-American sharecropper families also resided and toiled full time on Earl's farm. Like the millions of other poor sharecroppers, black and white, who lived in the South during Jimmy's childhood, Earl's sharecroppers paid him a share of their crops in return for the use of his land, seed, and tools and housing for themselves and their families. They lived in crude shacks near the fields they tilled. Like many Southern landowners of his era, Earl ran a store on his farm, which he stocked with food, soap, and other staples for the convenience of his sharecroppers and fieldhands. To avoid the long hike into town, Earl's customers willingly paid the inflated prices he charged for his goods. The high prices ensured that a healthy portion of the weekly wages he gave them would find its way back into his coffers.

HIS FATHER'S SON

Although Earl Carter was by far the most prosperous man in Archery, his family lived modestly. Their simple three-bedroom house had no running water or indoor toilet until Jimmy was 11 and no electricity until he was in his teens. Earl was cautious with his money. With the nation mired in the Great Depression (the economic downturn that struck the United States between 1929 and about 1940), he had reason to be. Thus, although Earl continued to expand his landholdings, the Carters enjoyed few luxuries. In stark contrast to the majority of their African-American neighbors, however, they never lacked for food, clothing, or other essentials.

Earl expected his oldest child to put in long hours toiling on the farm. Jimmy's chores included hauling water from the well, caring for the livestock, and chopping firewood. Often, his father would send him to the fields to pull weeds, turn sweet potato vines, or pick cotton alongside the farmhands. Mechanized power would not come to the farms of southwestern Georgia until Carter was an adult, so Jimmy used a mule-drawn plow to help break up the heavy red-clay soil for spring planting.

Although neighbors and schoolmates recalled that Jimmy had more chores than most boys in the community, the future president never tried to shirk his duties around the farm. For one thing, Earl was a stern disciplinarian who did not hesitate to use a whip to keep his son in line. For another, Jimmy was extremely anxious to please his father. Earl, Carter later recalled, "was the center of my life." One way Jimmy sought to win his father's approval was by setting up his own small business. On an acre of his father's land, Jimmy raised his own peanuts, then sold the boiled nuts for a nickel a bag on the streets of Plains. By the age of nine, Carter had earned enough from his peanut sales to purchase five bales of cotton, which he shrewdly stored for several years while the price of cotton rose.

Carter, however, often suspected that no matter what he accomplished, it would never be good enough for his demanding father: "I had strongly mixed feelings about him: of love, admiration, and pride, but also at least a retrospective concern about his aloofness from me," Jimmy later admitted. "I never remembered him saying, 'Good job,' ... or thanking me when I had done my best to fulfill one of his quiet suggestions that had the impact of orders."

BLACK AND WHITE

Despite his many chores, Jimmy still found time to have fun. He played tennis on the dirt court his father had laid out in the backyard, swam and trolled for catfish and eels in a nearby creek, hunted possums and other small game, and spent many contented hours just exploring the woods and fields near his house.

HOME: 1924–1953

Carter and His Father

In 1995, Jimmy Carter published a collection of original poems entitled *Always a Reckoning and Other Poems.* In "I Wanted to Share My Father's World," Carter examines his strained relationship with his demanding father, Earl Carter.

> This is a pain I mostly hide,
> but ties of blood, or seed, endure,
> and even now I feel inside
> the hunger for his outstretched hand,
> a man's embrace to take me in,
> the need for just a word of praise.
>
> I despised the discipline
> he used to shape what I should be,
> not owning up that he might feel
> his own pain when he punished me.
>
> I didn't show my need to him,
> since his response to an appeal
> would not have meant as much to me,
> or been as real.
>
> From those rare times when we did cross
> the bridge between us, the pure joy
> survives.
>
> I never put aside
> the past resentments of the boy
> until, with my own sons, I shared
> his final hours, and came to see
> what he'd become, or always was—
> the father who will never cease to be
> alive in me.

As a teenager, Jimmy (second from left in the top row) played on his high school basketball team. In his younger years, he often played with the children of the African Americans who worked on his father's land. As he got older, however, this was no longer accepted in his racially segregated society.

Carter often shared these pastimes with his young African-American neighbors, most of whom, like his best friend A.D., were the sons of his father's fieldhands. Given the widespread racial bigotry of his time and region, it seems remarkable that Jimmy's closest friends should have been African Americans. Yet, according to the traditions of the segregationist South, although whites and blacks were strictly separated in public institutions and facilities from schools to restrooms, white parents typically let their children have black playmates. However, when Southern boys and girls reached adolescence, segregation set in with a vengeance.

Thus, when Jimmy was 13 and big enough to drive his father's pickup truck into town (Georgia had no minimum driving age at that time), his new adolescent social life revolved around white friends. He escorted his girlfriends to the whites-only section of the movie theater in nearby Americus or for a milkshake at the whites-only soda fountain at the local drugstore. He shot hoops with his buddies on the all-white school basketball team and attended dances sponsored by the whites-only Baptist church. Jimmy still saw his African-American pals back in Archery from time to time, but the friendships of childhood had changed. His black friends now treated him differently. An incident that occurred when Jimmy was 14 symbolized this transformation. One day, when Jimmy and two black friends were out walking, they came upon a gate. To Jimmy's surprise, his companions held the gate open for him as he passed through. "Things were never again the same between them and me," Jimmy recalled. He admitted that at the time he did not question the change—it seemed to him that they were all just taking "one more step toward maturity"—a step toward the adult roles they knew they would be expected to assume in their racially segregated society.

THE INDEPENDENT MRS. CARTER

One of the few whites in the Plains and Archery communities who dared to cross the rigid racial lines of the period was Jimmy's mother. Although Lillian shrank from openly denouncing the political and social inequalities that existed between whites and African Americans during this era before the civil rights movement, she demonstrated by her actions her conviction that her black neighbors deserved the same level of medical care and friendly concern as her white ones.

Though most American women did not work outside of the home until much later in the twentieth century, Lillian was determined to continue her nursing career after her marriage. Throughout Jimmy's childhood, she worked at the hospital in Plains or as a private duty nurse. She also devoted countless hours to caring for Archery's African-American residents, who had no doctor to serve them. Lillian never charged her impoverished black neighbors for her time. And Earl, despite his own staunchly segregationist views, often quietly paid for the medicines his wife used in treating them. When

> "If you think in the right way you will develop: (1) the habit of accomplishing what you attempt, (2) the habit of expecting to like other people, (3) the habit of deciding quickly what you'd like to do and doing it, (4) the habit of sticking to it, (5) the habit of welcoming cheerfully all wholesome ideas and experiences, (6) a person who wants to build good mental habits should avoid the idle daydream; should give up worry and anger; hatred and envy; should neither fear nor be ashamed of anything that is honest and purposeful."
>
> — Just before starting high school, 13-year-old Jimmy recorded six "good mental health habits" in his scrapbook that he was determined to follow.

a black patient died, Lillian insisted on attending his or her funeral—a bold act in the segregated South.

While Lillian was off nursing, often working back-to-back shifts, Jimmy and his three siblings (Gloria, Ruth, born in 1929, and Billy, born in 1937) were cared for by a series of black housekeepers. Although Jimmy got along well with his sitters, he missed his mother. The "strong memory in my mind is coming home and my mother not being there," Jimmy would wistfully recall some six decades later.

GETTING AN EDUCATION

From the start, Jimmy excelled in school. Earl, who never went beyond the 10th grade, had high ambitions for his first born. His pet name for his oldest son was "Hot" (short for "hotshot"), and he was eager for Jimmy to earn top grades and go to college.

While Jimmy's African-American playmates attended crowded and understaffed schools in churches and private homes, Jimmy attended the all-white Plains High School. The school, despite its name, served grades one through eleven, and was, by all accounts, a remarkably good school for a small rural town. The high quality of the education offered at Plains High School owed much to the influence of its dedicated principal, Julia Coleman. Quickly recognizing Jimmy's superior intelligence and drive, Coleman encouraged him to join the debate team and read the great classics of Western literature.

When Jimmy graduated from high school in 1941, his goal was to gain admission to the U.S. Naval Academy in Annapolis, Maryland, and become a naval officer. Jimmy's uncle, Tom Gordy, was a lifelong navy man and was probably the chief reason for Carter's interest in the academy. Gordy faithfully sent Jimmy postcards and souvenirs from his far-flung travels, sparking in his young nephew visions of adventure and romance in exotic ports. Jimmy worried about meeting the Naval Academy's demanding physical requirements. Hoping to build up his slight physique and correct his flat arches, he put himself on a special banana diet and spent hours rolling his feet over Coke bottles. He also enlisted his father's help for the greatest hurdle a prospective Annapolis student faced—convincing his U.S. senators or local congressman to award him an appointment to the academy, a prerequisite for admission. Finally, after taking additional courses at a local junior college and at the Georgia Institute of Technology in Atlanta to make himself more competitive, Jimmy got his appointment. In June 1943, he boarded a train bound for Annapolis.

MARRIAGE AND A NAVAL CAREER
By the time Jimmy enrolled in the Naval Academy, the United States had been fighting in World War II for over a year, having entered the conflict following the Japanese bombing of Pearl Harbor in December 1941. Jimmy, therefore, was part of an accelerated wartime program

designed to train and graduate naval officers in three years instead of the usual four.

The Naval Academy proved challenging for Carter in ways he had never anticipated. Academically, he did well, ultimately graduating in the top 8 percent of his class. Carter also excelled in athletics and was, according to his coach, a cross-country runner of "great determination, stamina, and consistency." His social life, however, was another story. Older students frequently hazed underclassmen and Jimmy seems to have been a particular target of their ridicule and beatings. His slight build did not help him and neither did his toothy grin, one of Jimmy's trademarks since early childhood. "My problem is that I smile too much," Carter wrote in his diary, and he soon learned to put a grim expression on his face whenever he encountered an upperclassman in the corridors or dining hall.

Shortly after graduating from the Academy in 1946, Carter married 18-year-old Rosalynn Smith, his sister Ruth's best friend. Studious and shy, Rosalynn had long admired her friend's accomplished older brother. Jimmy first asked Rosalynn out in 1945 while he was home on leave. By the end of that first date, he knew he wanted to marry her.

The newlyweds settled in Norfolk, Virginia, where Carter served on a battleship being used to try out state-of-the-art equipment. World War II had ended in 1945, and Jimmy was frustrated by the limited opportunities for advancement in the scaled-down peacetime

After his graduation from the Naval Academy in 1946, Jimmy Carter married 18-year-old Rosalynn Smith, his sister Ruth's best friend. They settled in Norfolk, Virginia, where Jimmy was stationed. He soon became an officer on the U.S.S. *Sea Wolf,* a coveted position.

Navy. In 1948, he decided to apply for the Navy's elite submarine service. In 1952, following assignments in Hawaii, Connecticut, and California, he won a much sought-after post as senior officer of the U.S.S. *Sea Wolf*, one of the first nuclear-powered submarines. Carter's commanding officer was Hyman Rickover, the hard-driving creator of the nuclear submarine program. The brilliant admiral became a role model for Carter, who took to heart the blunt question Rickover asked him when he applied for the nuclear project. After Carter admitted in his interview that he had not always done his best at the Naval Academy, a disapproving Rickover wanted to know, "Why not?" Years later, Carter would use "Why Not the Best?" as a central slogan of his presidential campaign and the title of his campaign autobiography.

"WE'RE HOME"
Barely a year after winning the *Sea Wolf* assignment, Carter received a life-changing message: his father was dying of cancer. Carter immediately requested permission to leave so he could visit his ailing parent.

During his years away from his Southern community, Jimmy had adopted liberal racial views that stood in sharp contrast to Earl's segregationist beliefs, and since joining the Navy, Jimmy's infrequent visits home had often been tense. Yet when Carter returned home to sit by his father's deathbed, he found himself developing a new respect for Earl. Hundreds of visitors—black as well as white—called to bid farewell to the community patriarch, and many spoke of Earl's generosity toward them. Indeed, Carter was surprised to discover that his father had been secretly giving money and other aid to needy community members for years. Earl, he came to see, had been "an integral part of the community." Jimmy found himself longing for the stability and meaning his father's life now seemed to represent for him. He began to see tiny Plains as the ideal place for his family, which now included three sons—Jack, Chip, and Jeff (a daughter, Amy, would be born in 1967). He felt that in Plains they could fashion a community around themselves and enjoy the kind of lasting relationships they could never have if he remained in the Navy, where transfers were a way of life.

Thus, following his father's death in mid-1953, Carter resolved to resign his commission and head home. Reluctant to give up the travel and adventure that went with being a Navy wife, Rosalynn was bitterly disappointed. Jimmy, however, was adamant. Not only was he convinced his family would be better off in Plains, he also felt obliged to assist his mother. Lillian, who knew nothing about Earl's businesses, could not rely on her youngest son Billy, who was still in high school. Her daughters, Gloria and Ruth, were both married and living away from home.

Years later, Rosalynn Carter would describe her feelings during the car trip from Jimmy's final Naval assignment in New York to Georgia. "I became more and

Home: 1924–1953

more dejected the closer we got," Rosalynn remembered. "I didn't want to live in Plains. I had left there, moved on, and changed. But Jimmy was determined—and happy." As they drove into town, she recalled, he "turned to me with a smile and said cheerfully, 'We're home!'"

3

POLITICS: 1954–1976

NO SOONER HAD the Carters settled in Plains than they found themselves drawn into the racial turmoil that erupted in Georgia after the Supreme Court outlawed segregation in public schools in 1954. All across the South, outraged segregationists formed White Citizens Councils to resist school integration. At the same time, African Americans were organizing a national civil rights movement, devoted to achieving legal, political, and social equality for all United States citizens, regardless of race.

In Plains, the White Citizens Council was soon established under the leadership of the local police chief. When Carter, who firmly believed integration was the wave of the future, refused to

Politics: 1954–1976

After his father's death in 1953, Jimmy Carter decided to move his family, including his wife and sons Chip, Jack, and Jeff, back to Plains to help his mother with the family businesses. Soon after their arrival, segregation became an explosive issue. Jimmy supported integration and refused to join the White Citizens Council of Plains, an unpopular decision that caused an ineffective boycott of the family's peanut warehouse.

join, several council members visited him at his large downtown warehouse, where peanuts from local farmers were weighed and stored before they were shipped out to processors. Warning him his business would be boycotted if he did not cooperate, the men offered to pay Carter's five-dollar membership dues for him. "I would as soon flush five dollars down the toilet," Carter snapped. As it turned out, Jimmy's defiant attitude, although courageous, did not prove ruinous to his business. The warehouse boycott took place as threatened but only lasted a few months and only two of Carter's clients left him permanently over the controversy. A year later, Carter again stood up for his unpopular beliefs supporting integration when he, his family, and one other person were the only members of the Plains Baptist Church to vote in favor of admitting blacks to the congregation.

Carter's stint on the county school board from 1955 to 1962 also thrust him into the middle of the racial unrest that gripped the South during the 1950s and 1960s. Dedicated to improving the quality of education in his county, Jimmy spearheaded a movement to consolidate several local schools into one big high school. Since some people believed consolidation would hasten integration within the area's schools, Carter was branded a "race mixer and nigger lover." Ultimately, the movement failed at the polls.

STATE SENATOR

In 1962, with the peanut warehouse and farm he had inherited from his father prospering and his efforts to improve the local school system through consolidation frustrated, Carter decided he needed a fresh challenge. That October he announced his candidacy for the Democratic nomination for state senator. He embarked on a whirlwind 15-day campaign with virtually no funds and a staff consisting of his immediate family and a few friends.

Like many other districts in rural Georgia at that time, Carter's legislative district had a political "boss," who wielded enormous influence in deciding which candidates were elected. The district boss, Joe Hurst, preferred Carter's opponent. When it appeared Carter might win the primary, Hurst visited a local polling place and stuffed the ballot box with the ballots of hundreds of deceased "voters."

Losing by a razor-slim margin, an outraged Carter vowed to contest the election. Following weeks of effort, he finally persuaded a local judge to order a recount. The results of the primary election were reversed and Carter easily defeated his Republican opponent in the general election.

Carter served in the Georgia State Senate for four years, winning reelection in 1964. Devoting himself to his legislative duties, he painstakingly read every one of the approximately 900 bills that came before the Senate each session before voting on them. Unlike many senators, Carter consistently opposed the numerous "sweetheart" bills submitted each session on behalf of special-interest groups. Like most of his colleagues, however, he had little to say about Georgia's racial problems during his years in the Senate, preferring to avoid the highly charged integration issue for the time being.

COPING WITH DEFEAT
In June 1966, Carter made a surprise announcement: he was entering the Democratic primary for governor. Carter was undoubtedly heartened by the fact that few political commentators took seriously the man he considered as his chief rival. That man was Lester Maddox,

the owner of a popular Atlanta chicken restaurant. Maddox's claim to fame was an incident that had occurred at his whites-only eatery. When three black college students tried to be seated there, Maddox had threatened them with an ax handle. To Carter's dismay, Maddox, who had once called racial integration "un-American, un-Godly, and even criminal," not only beat him in the primary but actually became governor following the general election in November.

Deeply depressed, Carter turned to his sister Ruth, a Christian evangelist, for advice. Ruth, he later recalled, "urged me to react to failure and disappointment with . . . patience and wisdom" and to commit himself anew to his Christian faith. In time, Carter underwent a spiritual conversion that he would describe as being "born again." He also began studying the works of various theologians, scholars who write about God and God's relation to the universe. Carter was particularly drawn to the ideas of Reinhold Niebuhr, who argued that Christians should become involved in politics in order to improve their societies. "The sad duty of politics," Niebuhr had written, "is to establish justice in a sinful world."

A SECOND RUN FOR GOVERNOR

With a renewed sense of purpose, Carter reentered the political fray, announcing his candidacy for governor in the 1970 election. During the primary campaign, he set a grueling pace for himself and his staff, which now included

Politics: 1954–1976

two young Georgians destined to play important roles in his political career: Jody Powell and Hamilton Jordan.

Because Georgia law prohibits governors from serving consecutive terms, Maddox was not a candidate for governor in 1970. This time, Carter's main opponent in the Democratic primary was Carl Sanders, who had served as Georgia's governor from 1962 to 1966. Sanders, a wealthy Atlanta lawyer, enjoyed the support of the city's influential business establishment. Known to be relatively liberal on race issues, he was also popular among African Americans, who had been voting in larger numbers in Georgia since the passage of the Civil Rights Act of 1964. The act mandated equal access to public accommodations and empowered the attorney general to guarantee voting rights for every U.S. citizen.

During the campaign, Carter and his advisors crafted an image of Sanders as "Cufflinks Carl," a rich, big-city lawyer who had little interest in the blue-collar workers and farmers who comprised the bulk of Georgia's population. Carter, in contrast, was portrayed as a man of the people, a small-town business owner and farmer dedicated to serving the needs of ordinary citizens. Aware that many of these "ordinary citizens" were segregationists, Carter generally tried to skirt racial issues in his campaign. On occasion, he even made statements that seemed to court the racist vote. During the campaign, for example, Carter questioned a decision his opponent had made while serving as governor. At the time, Sanders had refused to let Governor George Wallace of Alabama, a die-hard segregationist, speak on

Georgia state property. Carter declared that he would, if elected, invite Wallace to speak in Georgia.

GOVERNOR CARTER

Carter's strategy of appealing to Georgia's large and predominantly white middle class proved successful. After defeating Sanders in the primary election, Carter went on to beat his Republican challenger in the general election in November. Three months later, on January 12, 1971, he was sworn in as governor. In his inaugural address,

---

Governor Carter's Inaugural Address

The following excerpts are from Governor Carter's inaugural address of January 12, 1971 in Atlanta, Georgia.

Our *people* are our most precious possession. We cannot afford to waste the talents and abilities given by God to one single person . . . . Every adult illiterate, every school drop-out, and every untrained retarded child is an indictment of us all. Our state pays a terrible and continuing human and financial price for these failures. It is time to end this waste. If Switzerland and Israel and other people can eliminate illiteracy, then so can we.

At the end of a long campaign, I believe I know our people as well as anyone. Based on the knowledge of Georgians north and south, rural and urban, liberal and conservative, I say to you quite frankly the time for racial discrimination is over . . . . No poor, rural, weak, or black person should ever have to bear the additional burden of being deprived of the opportunity of an education, a job, or simple justice.

Carter astounded many of his supporters and critics alike by declaring that the "time for racial discrimination is over." Leroy Johnson, Carter's sole black colleague in the state Senate during the early 1960s, was not surprised by the discrepancy between the new governor's speech and the tone of his recent campaign. "I understand why he ran that kind of ultraconservative campaign," said Johnson, because in Georgia "you ha[d] to do that to win."

As governor, Carter sought to distribute state aid to schools in wealthy and poor areas more equitably. He also appointed numerous blacks and women to state posts. However, the centerpiece of his administration was not social reform but reorganization of the state government. Committed to cutting waste in government, Carter streamlined Georgia's large network of state agencies and made them follow stringent new budgeting procedures. Georgians were impressed by their new governor's competency and integrity, but even some of Carter's strongest supporters believed he needed to make more of an effort to work with those legislators who disagreed with him.

NATIONAL AMBITIONS

Carter's liberal racial views as well as his program for consolidating Georgia's state agencies brought him national attention just months after he took office. In May 1971, Carter's picture appeared on the cover of *Time* magazine as a symbol of the new racially progressive

Jimmy Carter

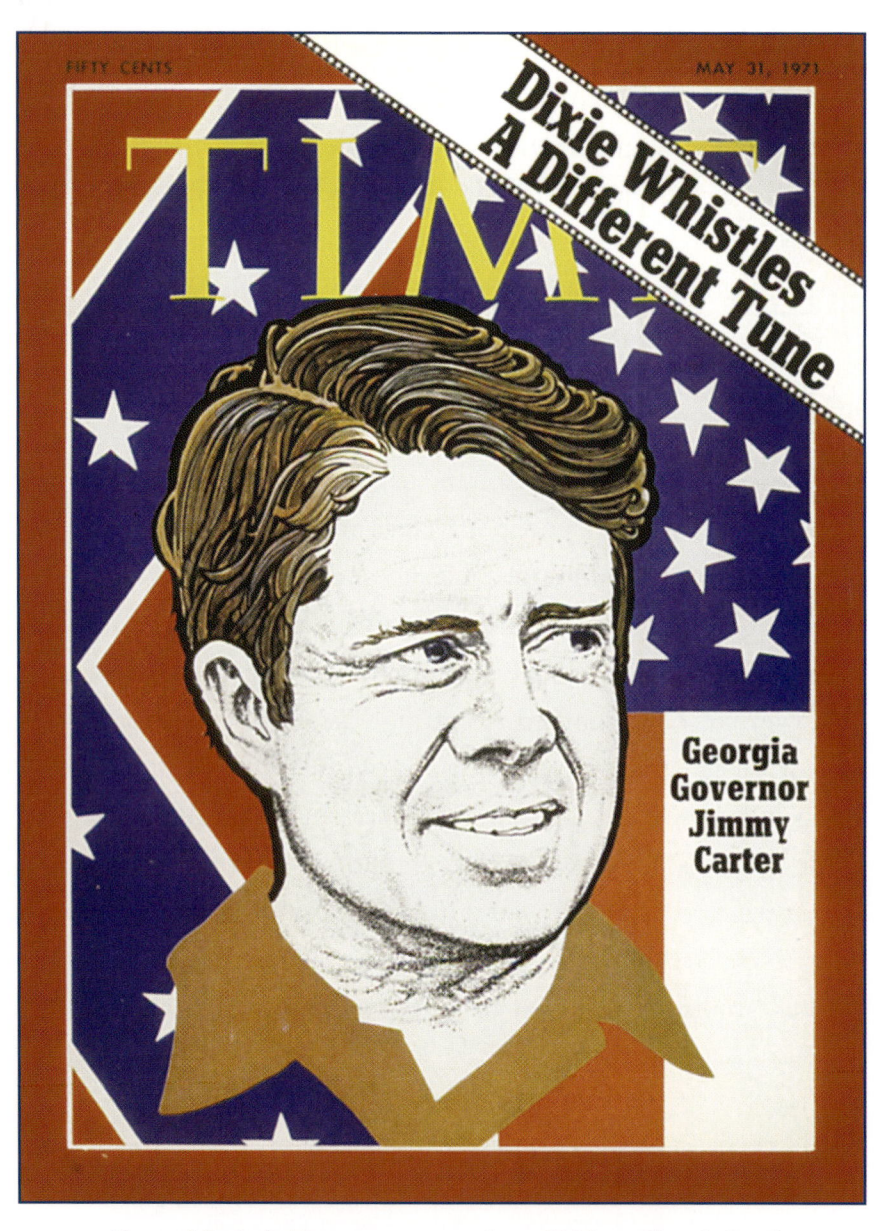

TIME — MAY 31, 1971 — FIFTY CENTS

Dixie Whistles A Different Tune

Georgia Governor Jimmy Carter

Many of Carter's ideas as governor brought him national attention. In May 1971, Carter appeared on the cover of *Time* representing the new racially progressive governors of the Deep South and also competent state government. The attention he received made Carter begin to think about running for president in 1976.

40

governors of the Deep South and of competent state government. Although the article hardly made Jimmy Carter a household name in America, Carter and his advisors were encouraged by the attention. They began thinking seriously about the upcoming presidential election.

The Democratic National Convention of July 1972 further convinced Carter and his closest aides—particularly Powell and Jordan—that a presidential run in 1976 was a reasonable plan, despite Carter's comparative lack of political experience and name recognition. Carter was thoroughly unimpressed by Senator George McGovern, the delegates' choice as their candidate for president in the 1972 election. Powell and Jordan were just as unimpressed by McGovern's advisors and were confident they could do at least as good a job of running a national campaign as the senator's staff was doing.

During the two years following the convention, a series of events took place in Washington, D.C., that would help Carter in his quest to win the 1976 nomination against more politically experienced competitors. In November 1972, Richard Nixon, the Republican incumbent, soundly defeated McGovern. Shortly before the election, however, a news story appeared regarding a break-in at the Democratic National Committee's headquarters in the Watergate Hotel complex in Washington. Over the next months, that seemingly minor incident would erupt into a full-scale scandal. "Watergate" would soon reach the highest levels of the Nixon administration, until even the president himself was under investigation for his alleged role in ordering, then trying to cover up, the break-in.

In August 1974, threatened with impeachment, Nixon became the first U.S. president to resign. He was succeeded by his recently-appointed vice president, Gerald Ford. Ford, the House minority leader, had been appointed vice president after Nixon's first vice president, Spiro Agnew, stepped down amidst charges that he had accepted bribes.

The American public was gravely disillusioned by the revelations of hush money, dirty campaign tricks, and huge, illegal campaign contributions that emerged during the course of the Watergate investigation. Carter and his advisors well understood the toll the scandal had taken on America's faith in its leaders. Particularly vulnerable were "career politicians" and "Washington insiders"—longtime senators and congressmen like Gerald Ford, for instance, who had served for nearly 25 years in the House of Representatives. Accordingly, Carter and his advisors decided to center their campaign on Carter's "outsider" status in the capital and on his unquestioned moral character.

WHY NOT THE BEST?

In December 1974—long before any other candidate threw his hat into the ring—Carter announced he would seek the Democratic nomination for president. Since few voters outside his home state were familiar with him, Carter's strategy was to run early and hard. Over the next few months, he visited nearly 40 states.

Carter also published a short autobiography in 1975,

hoping to introduce himself to the nation. Carter's book, *Why Not the Best?*, opened with the story of his interview with Rickover for the nuclear submarine program in which the admiral had demanded, "Why not?" when Carter admitted he had not always done his best in the Naval Academy. Applying Rickover's question to the

Why Not the Best?

The following are excerpts from Carter's introduction to his campaign autobiography, *"Why Not the Best?"* published in 1975:

As we observe the two hundredth birthday of our nation, it is appropriate to ask ourselves two basic questions: Can our government be honest, decent, open, fair, and compassionate? Can our government be competent?

As a matter of fact, many millions of American citizens have been asking these questions, and are doubtful about whether either can be answered in the affirmative. . . .

Does our government in Washington now represent accurately what the American people are, or what we ought to be? The answer is clearly, "No!" . . .

Our government can express the highest common ideals of human beings—if we demand of government true standards of excellence. . . .

It is now time to stop and to ask ourselves the question which my last commanding officer, Admiral Hyman Rickover, asked me and every other young naval officer in the atomic submarine program.

nation, Carter asked Americans why they should demand anything less than the best from their leadership. In the wake of the Watergate scandal, he wrote, Americans must ask themselves, "Can our government be honest, decent, open, fair, and compassionate?" Precisely because he was not part of the Washington "establishment," in contrast to President Ford and to most of his competitors for the Democratic nomination, Carter implied he was just the sort of leader who could provide the moral, just government Americans deserved. "*I would never tell a lie*," he promised repeatedly in his campaign speeches and advertisements.

With the assistance of his energetic "Peanut Brigade"—volunteers from Plains and elsewhere in Georgia—Carter campaigned especially hard in New Hampshire, the site of the first Democratic primary. The "Brigadiers" did such a good job of getting Carter's name and message of honest government out that Carter easily won the contest, defeating a host of other candidates who were better known nationally.

Building on the momentum of his success in New Hampshire, Carter went on to win most of the primaries. By July, when delegates arrived at the Democratic National Convention to select their candidate for president, his nomination was all but guaranteed. As his running mate, Carter chose Senator Walter Mondale of Minnesota, thereby ensuring that the Democratic ticket would represent both the North and South. Carter opened his acceptance speech with a line he had made famous over the last two years:

POLITICS: 1954–1976

On July 15, 1976, Jimmy Carter accepted the Democratic nomination for president. He chose Senator Walter Mondale of Minnesota as his running mate, thus ensuring that the Democratic ticket represented both the North and the South. He battled against Gerald Ford, the Republican nominee for the presidency.

"My name is Jimmy Carter and I'm running for president." When Carter first began introducing himself that way to the voting public in 1974, the typical response was, "Jimmy Who?" By 1976, very few Americans were asking that question. The one-term Georgia governor's rise to national prominence had been nothing less than meteoric.

A CLOSE CONTEST

Despite stiff competition from California's former governor, Ronald Reagan, Gerald Ford managed to win the Republican nomination. He faced an even tougher challenge in the national race. Ford had been severely criticized for pardoning Nixon shortly after his resignation. Many Americans also faulted the president for the country's economic woes, including high inflation and unemployment rates.

Not surprisingly, Carter began his campaign against Ford with a substantial lead in the opinion polls. Soon, however, as Ford hammered away at his opponent's "fuzziness" on the issues, Carter's standing in the polls began to slip. Indeed, Carter did tend to stress his moral character and distance from the scandal-ridden Washington community over specific issues. And to some observers, his economic and social views seemed contradictory. Carter, for instance, sounded conservative—even Republican—in his emphasis on reducing government spending; in his emphasis on helping the poor, blue-collar workers, farmers, and non-whites, however, he sounded liberal.

Also contributing to Carter's decline in the polls were some highly publicized remarks he made in an interview with the men's magazine, *Playboy*. Carter hoped the interview would show voters he was not some sort of "holier than thou" prude just because he was a devout Christian. As proof he did not consider himself superior to others, Carter stressed that although he had never been unfaithful to his wife, according to the moral standards of his religion, he was still a sinner. He explained that Christ had taught that "anyone who looks on a woman with lust has already committed adultery," adding, "I've committed adultery in my heart many times."

Politics: 1954–1976

The interview was a disaster. Secular Americans found Carter's talk of committing adultery in his heart strange—even laughable. Conservative Christians thought Carter should never have agreed to an interview with the risqué *Playboy* to begin with.

But just a month after Carter's ill-advised interview appeared in print, Ford made a far greater blunder. In a televised debate with Carter in October, Ford avowed there "was no Soviet domination of Eastern Europe and there never will be under a Ford administration." Since the Communist superpower, the Soviet Union, had dominated Eastern Europe for years, Ford's comments seemed to indicate to many Americans that he was alarmingly misinformed on basic foreign policy issues. Following the debate, Carter's downward slide in the polls halted abruptly.

On November 2, 1976, in one of the closest presidential races in American history, Carter won just over 50 percent of the popular vote and 297 electoral votes to Ford's 240. The man who had campaigned for the last two years as a Washington "outsider" was on his way to the White House.

4

High Expectations: 1977–1979

ON INAUGURATION DAY, January 20, 1977, instead of riding in the armored presidential limousine to the White House following his swearing-in ceremony at the Capitol, Jimmy Carter did something different: he walked the mile-long route up Pennsylvania Avenue to the White House. Through this simple yet deeply symbolic gesture, Carter hoped to show Americans that he intended to remain close to them—a president of and for the people.

Carter soon found other ways of demonstrating his resolve to be the "people's president." He sold the presidential yacht, ordered the Marine Corps band to stop playing "Hail to the Chief" at his public appearances, and sent his nine-year-old daughter Amy to a public

HIGH EXPECTATIONS: 1977–1979

Instead of riding in the traditional armored limousine from the Capitol to the White House, Jimmy Carter chose to walk the mile up Pennsylvania Avenue. With this and other actions, he demonstrated that he wanted to be the "people's president," a representative of the citizens of the nation.

school in Washington instead of an exclusive private one. He donned a homey sweater for a televised "fireside chat" with Americans about his high expectations for the coming year, expectations that included tax, educational, and welfare reform as well as a sweeping new national energy

Jimmy Carter

Excerpts from President Carter's Inaugural Speech of January 20, 1977

This inauguration ceremony marks a new beginning, a new dedication within our Government, and a new spirit among us all. A President may sense and proclaim that new spirit, but only a people can provide it.

Two centuries ago our Nation's birth was a milestone in the long quest for freedom, but the bold and brilliant dream which excited the founders of this Nation still awaits its consummation. I have no new dream to set forth today, but rather urge fresh faith in the old dream. . . .

The American dream endures. We must once again have full faith in our country and in one another. . . .

Let our recent mistakes bring a resurgent commitment to the basic principles of our Nation, for if we despise our own government we have no future. We recall in special times when we have stood briefly, but magnificently, united. In those times no prize was beyond our grasp.

But we cannot dwell upon remembered glory. We cannot afford to drift. We reject the prospect of failure or mediocrity or an inferior quality of life for any person. Our Government must at the same time be both competent and compassionate.

We have already found a high degree of personal liberty, and we are now struggling to enhance equality of opportunity. Our commitment to human rights must be absolute, our laws fair, our natural beauty preserved; the powerful must not persecute the weak, and human dignity must be enhanced.

We have learned that "more" is not necessarily "better," that even our great Nation has its recognized limits, and that we can neither answer all questions nor solve all problems. We cannot afford to do everything, nor can we afford to lack boldness as we meet the future. So, together, in a spirit of individual sacrifice for the common good, we must simply do our best. . . .

policy. To help realize this last aim, Carter announced the formation of a cabinet-level Department of Energy.

The American public's response to their new president's unassuming style and ambitious domestic program was overwhelmingly positive. By spring, Carter's approval rating was an impressive 75 percent. But there were signs of impending trouble for the Washington newcomer. Most centered on his relations with Capitol Hill.

CARTER VERSUS CONGRESS

Since Carter's own party held large majorities in both the Senate and House, it seemed as though the president should have been able to work well with Congress. Nonetheless, Carter's relationship with the legislative branch was strained from the start. He had, after all, campaigned as an outsider devoted to challenging the sway of Washington's "career politicians," a label many longtime legislators—even Congress's most prominent Democrats, House Speaker "Tip" O'Neill and Senator Edward Kennedy, could not help but suspect included them. To make matters worse, Carter declared that if members of Congress refused to back his initiatives, he would go over their heads. He would, he announced, appeal directly to the people, who would pressure their representatives into supporting his proposals.

Convinced he could bypass Congress to achieve his policy goals and contemptuous of the dealmaking and backslapping of traditional politics, the new president made little effort to build alliances in the House and

Senate. Carter's White House staff, which should have helped smooth his way with Congress, only added to his problems on the Hill. Carter, realizing that he needed the help of experienced politicians, had appointed many Washington "insiders" to his cabinet, such as Secretary of State Cyrus Vance and Secretary of Health, Education and Welfare Joseph Califano. But most of his top staff, including his press secretary, Jody Powell, and closest aide, Hamilton Jordan, were fellow Georgians who had little understanding of—or liking for—the Washington "establishment."

Further complicating Carter's relationship with Congress was the gap between his own moderate political beliefs and the views of the Democratic Party's large and influential liberal wing. Carter, who was deeply committed to advancing gender and racial equality, pleased the liberals by appointing unprecedented numbers of blacks, Hispanics, and women to federal judgeships and senior government posts. For example, he appointed a woman, Juanita Kreps, as Secretary of Commerce, and he asked a black Georgian legislator, Andrew Young, to serve as America's ambassador to the United Nations. However, his determination to balance the budget and reduce the $66 billion federal deficit he had inherited from President Ford, even if that meant cutting back social programs, infuriated many congressional Democrats. And over the course of Carter's term in office, the rift between the president and liberal Democrats over federal spending on welfare, job training, and other costly social programs would only grow.

HIGH EXPECTATIONS: 1977–1979

FOCUSING ON ENERGY

Carter's troubled relations with Congress handicapped his efforts to get his legislative program enacted. A striking example of the lack of cooperation between the president and Congress was the national energy policy initiative Carter had put at the top of his long list of proposals. Three years before Carter's election, the country had endured an energy crisis. A coalition of oil-exporting nations in the Middle East, home to two-thirds of the world's oil reserves, had slapped an oil embargo on the United States for supporting Israel against its Arab neighbors in the Yom Kippur War. Confronted with widespread fuel shortages and skyrocketing gasoline prices, Americans had agreed something had to be done to reduce the nation's dependence on foreign oil. In 1974, however, when an Israeli-Arab cease-fire led to a lifting of the embargo and a return to the abundant oil supplies of the past, most of the complaints regarding America's energy practices abruptly stopped.

But if the American public had all but abandoned the idea of reforming the nation's energy policies by 1977, Carter had not. He remained profoundly concerned about both the domestic and international consequences of U.S. reliance on foreign oil, a dependence that had actually grown since the Arab embargo. In 1977, America imported nearly half its oil—up from about one-third before the embargo—and consumed significantly more fossil fuel than any other nation on the globe. Carter believed that if Americans did not change their habits, periodic fuel shortages and price hikes were inevitable. Moreover, he worried that overdependence on foreign oil threatened national security. Oil-producing nations, particularly in the politically unstable Middle East, could use their oil reserves as a powerful economic weapon against the United States. They had already done so during the Yom Kippur War and Carter believed they would not hesitate to do so again.

In April 1977, therefore, Carter submitted an energy package to Congress designed to promote American energy independence. Carter's program called for increased government spending for alternative energy development, including solar and nuclear power. It also proposed tax incentives to encourage Americans to conserve natural gas and oil. For example, people would receive tax breaks for better insulating their homes or for purchasing smaller, more fuel-efficient cars. The program also called for the gradual lifting of the federal price ceilings on domestic natural gas and oil, established during the Nixon administration. Carter believed that federal price controls, which kept the prices of these fuels artficially low, had given American consumers little incentive to conserve fuel and American producers little incentive to develop alternative energy technologies. Among the other features of Carter's energy package were a federal tax on industries and utilities that burned natural gas or oil and stronger federal energy efficiency standards for new cars and buildings.

"THE MORAL EQUIVALENT OF WAR"

Carter had made little effort to involve legislators in the creation of his energy proposal. When he finally sat down

HIGH EXPECTATIONS: 1977–1979

Jimmy Carter often had a combative relationship with Congress, which created a problem for him when he wanted to pass his energy proposal. Speaker of the House Thomas P. ("Tip") O'Neill was a supporter, and helped by creating a special ad hoc committee to review the proposal in the House, but Carter had no such help in the Senate.

with Speaker O'Neill to review the package, therefore, the president was shocked to discover that getting the bill through the House would be a greater challenge than he had imagined. Carter's complex package would have to be routed through well over a dozen different committees and subcommittees. O'Neill warned him that each of these could be expected to take the ax to one or another of the program's provisions. The Speaker, however, loyally came to the president's rescue by creating a special Ad Hoc Committee on Energy to review the entire package. By the end of the summer, O'Neill had managed to push Carter's program through the House without major revisions.

Getting the legislation through the Senate was another

story. Majority Leader Robert Byrd refused to create a special committee to review the package in its entirety. Instead, he divided the legislation among several committees, each of which fought long and hard over the program's various components. As the Senate battle dragged on, lobbyists from special-interest groups, including the oil and automobile industries, pressured committee members to revise the legislation to serve their clients' particular needs.

In the meantime, Carter appealed to the people to back his program. But the public was unmoved by Carter's dramatic description of his energy crusade as "the moral equivalent of war." In fact, the phrase, whose unfortunate acronym was "MEOW," made critics scoff. Convinced Carter was overstating the nation's energy problem, most Americans were reluctant to adopt the lifestyle changes he urged. There was little public support for carpooling, purchasing smaller automobiles, or turning thermostats down a few degrees. Consequently, any dreams Carter may have harbored of American voters pressuring their representatives to support his energy legislation went unfulfilled.

Finally, in October 1978, eighteen months after Carter had announced his program, his energy legislation passed both houses of Congress. Carter's victory, however, was far from complete, for his original proposal had been seriously weakened. Although Congress lifted the price ceilings on natural gas, it rejected Carter's proposals to boost the price of domestic oil and to tax industries using oil and natural gas. Legislators also significantly reduced his "gas-guzzler" tax on the purchase of automobiles that had poor gas mileage.

High Expectations: 1977–1979

THE PANAMA CANAL TREATIES

Carter soon found himself battling Congress over foreign policy issues. His first big foreign policy struggle with Capitol Hill centered on the Central American country of Panama, and more specifically, on the Panama Canal, the waterway that links the Atlantic and Pacific Oceans across the narrow Isthmus of Panama.

For economic and strategic reasons, President Theodore Roosevelt had authorized the building of the interoceanic waterway in 1903. That same year, Panamanian officials granted the United States exclusive control over the canal and the surrounding zone in return for U.S. support in Panama's ongoing struggle against its former ruler, the South American nation of Colombia. Over time, however, Panamanians became increasingly resentful of American control of the Canal Zone. During the mid-1960s, widespread anti-American rioting in Panama convinced President Lyndon Johnson to begin negotiating a new canal treaty. Presidents Nixon and Ford continued the process, but their efforts were stalled by domestic critics. Among these was Ford's popular opponent in the 1976 Republican primaries, Ronald Reagan, who insinuated that relinquishing the canal would make the United States look weak, particularly in the wake of its recent defeat in the Vietnam War.

Carter, however, resolved to forge ahead with the negotiations. As Vice President Mondale would later say, Jimmy Carter was much more concerned with doing what he believed to be right than with what might be best for him politically. Eager to improve relations between the United States and Latin America, Carter understood that for many of America's neighbors to the south, U.S. control of the canal had come to symbolize Yankee dominance and meddling in their region. Moreover, Carter worried that if the protests against U.S. authority in the Canal Zone escalated into armed conflict, American ships could lose access to the waterway altogether. Therefore, in September 1977, Carter signed two treaties with Panama. Under the terms of these treaties, the United States would relinquish the canal to Panamanian control by the year 2000, and Panama would permanently guarantee the waterway's neutrality thereafter. Carter now had to convince the Senate to ratify the treaties.

The president knew his task would not be easy. Congressional conservatives were already angry with Carter for pardoning virtually all Vietnam War draft resisters on his first full day in office. Carter hoped the pardon would help heal the wounds of the controversial and unpopular war, but many right wingers believed the draft evaders should be prosecuted, not forgiven. Consequently, Carter's conservative opponents in the Senate were raring for a fight. When he submitted the canal treaties for their approval, for eight long months they blasted away at the agreements as a spineless "giveaway" of U.S. property. Finally in April 1978, following intensive lobbying by the administration, the treaties won the two-thirds majority required for ratification, but only by a razor-slim margin.

HIGH EXPECTATIONS: 1977–1979

Jimmy Carter and Omar Torrijos signed the Panama Canal Treaty in September 1977, guaranteeing that control of the Panama Canal would be relinquished to Panama by the year 2000. Thereafter, Panama would ensure that the canal remained neutral. The treaties were narrowly ratified by Congress in April 1978.

HUMAN RIGHTS AND INTERNATIONAL RELATIONS

One of the reasons Carter had sought to renegotiate the Panama Canal treaties was that he viewed returning the Canal Zone to Panama as a matter of fairness. And treating other nations and peoples with justice and respect was an essential element of Carter's chief foreign policy goal: the advancement of human rights throughout the world. For too long, Carter believed, U.S. foreign policy had focused on achieving and maintaining superiority over Communist nations—and particularly the principal Communist power, the Soviet Union (USSR). No longer, he vowed would an "inordinate fear of communism" drive the United States to "embrace any dictator who joined us in that fear." Instead, his administration's foreign policy would strive to reflect the best in America's national character: an unwavering commitment to justice, freedom, and equality. "I feel very deeply that when people are put in prison without trails, and tortured and deprived of basic human rights that the President of the United States ought to have the right to express displeasure and to do something about it," Carter asserted. He declared that his concern with human rights was rooted in his own experiences witnessing the civil rights struggles of the 1950s and 1960s in the South.

As part of his human rights crusade, Carter cut U.S. military and economic assistance to Ethiopia, Argentina, and Chile, among other countries, on the grounds that these countries' dictatorial rulers had violated their citizens' fundamental rights. In contrast, he increased aid to other countries because of their progress in ensuring their citizens fair trials and promoting freedom of speech, assembly, and religion. But Carter found it impossible to apply his human rights-based policy evenly, and his critics were quick to point this out. For instance, Carter continued to support the autocratic shah (king) of Iran, America's longtime ally in the politically unstable and oil-rich Middle East. For strategic reasons, he also exempted the large and powerful People's Republic of China (PRC) from his human rights campaign, even though the Communist regime established on mainland China in 1949 was among the most repressive in the world. Indeed, in January 1979, Carter established full diplomatic relations with the PRC, completing the long process of détente (relaxation of political tension) with Communist China begun by Nixon seven years earlier.

CARTER AND THE SOVIET UNION
Carter did not, however exempt the chief Communist power in the world from his human rights crusade. Influenced by his strongly anti-Soviet national security advisor, Zbigniew Brzezinski, Carter denounced the Soviet Union's leaders for flagrant human rights violations and for refusing to tolerate political dissent. Soviet officials were particularly offended when Carter publicly praised Russian dissident Andrei Sakharov and urged him to continue his courageous struggle for human rights in his homeland. Carter, the Communist leadership believed, was meddling in their internal affairs solely to embarrass them, and they told him in no uncertain terms to mind his own business.

But while Carter did not hesitate to chastise the Soviets for their poor human rights record, he was committed to continuing the arms-control negotiations with the Soviet Union begun under the administrations of Nixon and Ford. The huge nuclear arsenals assembled by the United States and the Soviet Union during the past three decades as part of their costly "cold war" competition for global supremacy dismayed Carter. The president sent Secretary of State Vance to Moscow in March 1977 to suggest further cuts in the preliminary SALT II (Strategic Arms Limitations Talks) pact negotiated by the Ford administration. The secretary of state received a cool response from President Leonid Brezhnev and his colleagues, who were still smarting from Carter's support of the dissident Sakharov.

Carter persisted, and eventually the Soviets agreed to resume the SALT talks. Negotiations progressed slowly, but in June 1979, Brezhnev and Carter finally signed a treaty limiting both nations to a total of about 2,000 "delivery vehicles" (submarine-based missiles, intercontinental ballistic missiles, and long-range bombers). The treaty also restricted the number of warheads each country could have and the development of new types of nuclear armaments.

Carter now faced the same hurdle with SALT II that he had confronted after signing the Panama Canal treaties— winning Senate ratification. Since many legislators opposed the treaty for allegedly favoring the Soviets, the administration prepared for a long battle. To Carter's disappointment, as the end of 1979 approached, SALT II was still stalled in the Senate and its prospects for ratification appeared poor.

BROKERING PEACE BETWEEN ISRAEL AND EGYPT
During the same period that Carter was struggling to convince first the Soviets, and then the Senate, to back SALT II, he achieved what most historians agree was his greatest foreign policy success: brokering a peace agreement between Israel and Egypt. Since 1948, when the Jewish State of Israel was established within the former British protectorate of Palestine, the Middle East had been plagued by four Arab-Israeli wars, terrorism, and the pressing dilemma of what to do with millions of embittered Arab-Palestinian

refugees. Promoting peace in the volatile Middle East, and particularly between Israel and its most powerful Arab neighbor, Egypt, had been one of Carter's chief foreign policy goals from the start. Consequently, soon after taking office, Carter began talking with Israeli leader Menachem Begin and Egyptian leader Anwar el-Sadat.

PRESIDENT CARTER'S LEGACY
Peace between Egypt and Israel

The Egyptian-Israeli Peace Treaty of 1979 is generally considered the greatest legacy of Jimmy Carter's presidency. Most scholars agree that Carter's role in achieving the treaty—the first ever between Israel and any Arab nation—was a significant diplomatic achievement.

After just three meetings at the Camp David peace summit convened by Carter in 1978, Israeli Prime Minister Menachem Begin and Egyptian President Anwar el-Sadat were barely on speaking terms. Determined to salvage the talks, Carter made a bold decision. If the two leaders would not communicate directly with one another, they would have to communicate through him. With painstaking attention to detail, he helped compose a peace proposal for Begin and Sadat's review. Shuttling back and forth between the two men, Carter at last secured their approval on day 13 of the summit.

Carter's impressive grasp of details, problem-solving skills, and sheer doggedness all contributed enormously to the success of the Israeli-Egyptian peace talks. Thus, many people were dismayed when Carter was not awarded the Nobel Peace Prize for 1979 along with Begin and Sadat. The Nobel Committee later explained that Carter had not been nominated in time for their deadline. In 2002, Carter was finally awarded the Nobel Peace Prize for his tireless promotion of international peace and human rights before and after leaving the White House. As the committee declared, his "mediation was a vital contribution" to the treaty signed between Egypt and Israel more than 20 years earlier.

JIMMY CARTER

Since the establishment of the State of Israel in 1948, tension between Jews and Arabs in the Middle East had caused significant unrest. Jimmy Carter's work for peace led him to begin talks with Anwar el-Sadat of Egypt (right) and Menachem Begin of Israel (left), resulting first in the Camp David Accords in 1977 and then the signing of the formal Arab–Israeli Treaty in 1979, pictured here.

In November 1977, Sadat made an historic trip to Jerusalem to underscore his own commitment to achieving peace. Over the following months, however, Israeli and Egyptian peace negotiations stalled. The main sticking point was the critical issue of Israeli occupation of the Sinai Peninsula, which Israel had seized from Egypt during the Six Day War of 1967 and which Egypt had tried—and failed—to win back in the Yom Kippur War of 1973.

With the negotiations deadlocked, Carter proposed a novel idea: face-to-face talks between Prime Minister Begin and President Sadat at Camp David, the presidential retreat in Maryland, with himself as mediator. The two leaders accepted, and in early September 1978, they and their negotiating teams arrived at Camp David.

The tense and complex negotiations dragged on for nearly two weeks and were saved only by Carter's astute and dogged intervention between the two longtime enemies. Finally, on day 13, Begin and Sadat announced that they had agreed on a framework for a peace treaty. Under the terms of this treaty, Israel would relinquish the Sinai Peninsula in exchange for Egyptian recognition of Israel's right to exist in peace. Additionally, these "Camp David Accords" included a blueprint for broader peace negotiations in the Middle East that would address the right of Arab-Palestinian refugees to self-government in the Israeli-occupied territories of the West Bank and Gaza.

Several more months of "shuttle diplomacy," with Carter jetting between Sadat in Cairo and Begin in Jerusalem, resulted in a formal Egyptian-Israeli Peace Treaty in 1979. The historic agreement, the first peace treaty ever between Israel and an Arab nation, was signed on March 26 during a ceremony hosted by Carter at the White House. Carter was widely praised for his crucial role in brokering peace between Israel and Egypt. But by the spring of 1979, as he struggled to cope with a series of difficult political and economic challenges at home, his popularity with the American public was sinking.

5

"A Crisis of Confidence": 1979–1981

BY 1979, CARTER had developed a serious image problem. Fairly or not, a growing number of Americans viewed the president as ineffectual. Carter had achieved many of his legislative goals. He had established a Department of Education and had reformed the civil service; he had lifted burdensome federal regulations on the transportation and banking industries and had halted production of the costly B-1 bomber. Nonetheless, much of his vast program wound up gutted by Congress or caught up in one House or Senate committee or another. Because he had set such an ambitious domestic agenda for his administration (including welfare, tax, educational, urban, and health reform), for many Americans, Carter's substantial

A Crisis of Confidence: 1979–1981

By 1979, Carter's reputation was faltering. He was seen as being generally ineffectual. He had met several of his goals, particularly in regard to education, but he had set many others that had not been accomplished. His image also suffered when Bert Lance, the director of the Office of Management and Budget was accused of financial misdealings.

legislative accomplishments were overshadowed by what he had *not* achieved. "Everybody has warned me not to take on too many projects so early in the administration, but it's almost impossible for me to delay something that I see needs to be done," the president admitted in his diary.

In addition to trying to do too much too quickly, the president's critics charged, Carter tended to become caught up in the smallest details of his wide-ranging agenda. Carter's detractors, particularly those in the media, also raised doubts regarding his character by focusing an enormous amount of attention on the "Lance Affair." Late in 1977, Bert Lance, the director of the Office of Management and Budget and Carter's close friend, resigned after being accused of financial misdealings. Although the president's friend was eventually cleared of all wrongdoing, the Lance Affair nonetheless damaged Carter's squeaky-clean image.

AN ENERGY PANIC AND A WEAKENING ECONOMY

During the winter and spring of 1979, two interrelated domestic issues took an even heavier toll on Carter's standing with the public: an energy crisis and an increasingly troubled economy. The second major energy crisis of the 1970s began in January 1979 when Muslim fundamentalists in Iran overthrew the shah and that nation was plunged into political and economic chaos. With Iran's fuel exports halted, OPEC (Organization of Petroleum Exporting Countries), an alliance of Middle Eastern oil-producing nations, seized the opportunity to raise oil prices dramatically. As in 1973, disgruntled Americans endured long lines and high prices at the gasoline pump. Even worse, the new energy panic had a devastating effect on the economy. Soaring oil prices led to ballooning inflation rates, while fuel shortages led to production cutbacks in American factories and more unemployment.

A Crisis of Confidence: 1979–1981

By summer, Carter's public approval ratings had dipped below 30 percent. In response, the president convened a ten-day "domestic summit" at Camp David to reevaluate his administration's policies and goals. Immediately following the summit, the president made what was destined to become the most famous speech of his political career. In a televised address on July 15, Carter outlined several proposals aimed at meeting America's newest energy crisis. These included abolishing federal ceilings on domestic oil prices and a "windfall profits" tax on U.S. oil companies to deter price gouging. Carter also wanted to raise revenues for solar energy and synthetic fuel research. In the wake of a recent near-catastrophic accident at the Three Mile Island nuclear plant in Pennsylvania, Carter, who had previously viewed nuclear energy as a partial solution to America's energy woes, was no longer stressing nuclear power as an alternative energy source.

But the president did not limit his July 15 address to the issue of energy. Rejecting the counsel of many of his closest advisors, including Vice President Mondale, Carter decided to tackle broader issues in his speech. Americans, Carter declared, were suffering from something far graver than an energy crisis: they were in the grips of a spiritual crisis. Over the last decade, a series of demoralizing events, including the Watergate scandal, military defeat in Vietnam, and two energy panics, had robbed Americans of their traditional faith in their government and even in the future itself. Coupled with this "crisis of confidence," Carter said, was a widespread longing for a sense of "meaning." He argued that

President Carter's "Malaise Speech"

The following excerpts are from Carter's so-called "Malaise Speech" of July 15, 1979:

I want to talk to you . . . about a fundamental threat to American democracy. . . . It is a crisis of confidence. . . .

The confidence that we have always had as a people is not simply some romantic dream or a proverb in a dusty book that we read just on the Fourth of July.

It is the idea which founded our Nation and has guided our development as a people. Confidence in the future has supported everything else—public institutions and private enterprise, our own families, and the very Constitution of the United States. . . . We've always believed in something called progress. We've always had a faith that the days of our children would be better than our own.

Our people are losing that faith, not only in government itself, but in their ability as citizens to serve as the ultimate rulers and shapers of our democracy. As a people we know our past and are proud of it. . . . But just as we are losing our confidence in the future, we are also beginning to close the door on our past.

In a nation that was proud of hard work, strong families, close-knit communities, and our faith in God, too many of us now tend to worship self-indulgence and consumption. Human identity is no longer defined by what one does, but by what one owns. But we've discovered that owning things and consuming things does not satisfy our longing for meaning. We've learned that piling up material goods cannot fill the emptiness of lives which have no confidence or purpose . . .

many Americans had lost sight of the moral ideals on which their nation rested and had begun, instead, to "worship self-indulgence and consumption." Governmental efforts to meet the current energy and economic problems, he warned, were merely short-term fixes. "All the legislation in the world can't fix what's wrong with America," he asserted, until its citizens "faced the truth" of their "deeper" crisis and determined to rekindle their flickering faith—"faith in each other, faith in our ability to govern ourselves, and faith in the future of this nation."

Carter's listeners were dismayed by his brutally frank appraisal of their spiritual condition. Critics began scornfully referring to Carter's address as the "Malaise Speech," although the president never actually used the word "malaise" (meaning psychological unease). Carter's already dismal approval ratings fell even farther when he followed his speech by dismissing several top advisors, including his treasury and energy secretaries. Carter hoped the purge would restore confidence in his administration; instead it left the public with greater doubts than ever about his leadership abilities.

CRISES IN IRAN AND AFGHANISTAN

In late 1979, two major foreign crises added to Carter's woes. The first occurred in Iran. Since the previous winter, when the shah had been overthrown, Iran's government had been under the control of an anti-Western Muslim cleric, Ayatollah Khomeini. On November 4, just weeks after Carter permitted the cancer-ridden shah to enter the

In 1979, anti-American protests, including the burning of the American flag, broke out in Tehran, Iran. Carter had allowed the shah of Iran to enter the United States for treatment for cancer. The protesters offered hostages taken from the United States embassy in Tehran in exchange for the return of the overthrown shah, whom they wanted to stand trial in his homeland.

United States for medical treatment, thousands of angry Iranian college students stormed the U.S. embassy in Tehran, Iran's capital, taking more than 60 Americans hostage. Although one ailing hostage and most of the black and female hostages were released, the students, with the ayatollah's blessing, demanded that the shah be returned to Iran to stand trial in exchange for the remaining 52 captives. Short of handing over the shah or taking military action, which almost surely would have resulted in the execution of the hostages, there was little Carter and his advisors could do to resolve the problem. Iranian bank accounts in the United States were frozen, official diplomatic ties with Tehran were severed, and secret negotiations were arranged. As the crisis dragged on with no end in sight, the hostages became a national obsession. Each evening on the national news, Americans watched in frustration as Iranian students, chanting "death to America," burned U.S. flags or paraded blindfolded hostages before the ever-present television cameras. The pressure on Carter was nearly unbearable. As he later recalled, "The first week of November 1979 marked the beginning of the most difficult period of my life. The safety and wellbeing of the American hostages became a constant concern for me, no matter what other duties I was performing as President. I would walk in the White House gardens early in the morning and lie awake at night, trying to think of additional steps I could take to gain their freedom without sacrificing the honor and security of our nation."

In late April, nearly six months after the embassy takeover, a desperate Carter finally authorized a military rescue mission over the objections of Secretary of State Vance, who believed the operation was too risky. The mission was aborted after an equipment failure in the desert outside Tehran. Tragically, in the process of pulling out, two aircraft collided in a sandstorm, killing eight U.S. soldiers. The next day, Carter informed the American people of the failed mission, for which he took complete responsibility. Interpreting the ill-fated rescue attempt as just another sign of his fundamental ineptitude, Carter's critics had little sympathy for the beleaguered president. Vance, his own secretary of state, resigned in protest.

In the meantime, Carter was confronted with another major international crisis. Hoping to prop up Afghanistan's failing Communist regime, Soviet troops invaded the country on Christmas Day 1979. Some Western observers suspected that control over the oil-rich and strategically vital Persian Gulf region was the Soviet leadership's true objective in invading and occupying Afghanistan.

Reacting forcefully to the invasion, Carter announced an embargo on grain sales to the Soviet Union, a U.S. boycott of the upcoming Olympics Games in Moscow, a significant increase in the defense budget for the coming year, and the withdrawal of the SALT II treaty from Senate consideration. In his State of the Union Address of January 1980, Carter also introduced the "Carter Doctrine" for U.S. protection of the Persian Gulf. "An attempt by any outside force to gain control of the Persian Gulf region will be regarded as an assault on the vital interests of the United States of America," he declared, "and such an assault will be repelled by any means necessary, including military force." The Soviets, however, stubbornly resisted Carter's efforts to pressure them into withdrawing from Afghanistan. (As it turned out, Soviet troops remained in Afghanistan until 1989, when the Soviet Union finally abandoned its costly decade-long battle to subdue the determined Afghan rebel forces.)

THE 1980 PRESIDENTIAL CAMPAIGN

In late 1979, already a trying year for Carter, things became even more difficult when Senator Edward Kennedy of

Massachusetts announced he would be seeking the Democratic presidential nomination. In what came to be known as his "Rose Garden strategy" (after the famous White House garden), Carter vowed to stay in Washington and focus on the hostage crisis rather than actively campaign for the upcoming 1980 primaries. Although Carter's popularity rating was low and organized labor and many liberals favored Kennedy, the Massachusetts senator was tainted by a scandalous past and his campaign soon floundered. After defeating Kennedy in most of the primaries, Carter was able to secure renomination on the first ballot at the Democratic National Convention. Nonetheless, Kennedy's challenge of a sitting president and the drawn-out battle against his own party's incumbent from November 1979 right up to the convention in August 1980 had left the Democrats divided and weakened as they entered the national election. Carter's Republican opponent in the November election was to be the conservative Ronald Reagan, former governor of California and outspoken critic of the Panama Canal treaties.

Embarrassing revelations regarding his brother Billy's financial dealings with the Libyan dictator and sworn enemy of the United States, Mu'ammar al-Gadhafi, troubled Carter early in the national campaign. A far greater political liability for Carter than his younger brother was the U.S. economy, which was beset by an annual inflation rate of more than 12 percent (up from 6 percent in 1976), mounting interest rates, and high unemployment. Carter had tried a number of different remedies for the ailing economy, from voluntary wage and price controls to pressuring Congress to curb governmental spending. But nothing seemed to help for long, and the business establishment and general public alike tended to pin the blame for the country's economic troubles squarely on the president.

The Iranian crisis further cut into Carter's popular support. As the 12-month anniversary of the embassy seizure approached, the 52 hostages still languished in Tehran. Although the shah died of cancer in July and the expansionist Iraqi dictator Saddam Hussein invaded Iran in September, the Americans' captors stubbornly refused to hand them over. Implying Carter was a weak commander in chief, Reagan proclaimed that, if elected, *he* would use military force against international terrorists.

Reagan's substantial lead in the polls narrowed for a time in early autumn, after the economy showed some modest signs of improvement and the Carter team made a point of publicizing some of the more extreme opinions Reagan had voiced in the past. (Reagan, for example, had once said that "fascism" was the real basis of President Franklin Roosevelt's New Deal). But the televised debate between Reagan and Carter on October 28 soon turned the tide again toward Reagan, whose training as a movie actor helped him excel on television. In contrast, Carter appeared tense and stiff on camera. Reagan's closing statement was especially damaging to the president. Pointing to what he called Carter's high "misery index" (the unemployment rate plus the inflation rate), Reagan looked directly into the television monitor and asked his audience, "Are you better off than you were four years ago?" Many voters decided they were not.

On November 4, election day, voter turnout was low. Just 52 percent of registered voters chose to take part in the election, which coincidentally fell on the one-year anniversary of the embassy takeover in Tehran. When the results were in, Reagan had won by a landslide, polling 51 percent of the popular vote to Carter's 41 percent. A third party candidate, John Anderson of Illinois, polled 7 percent. Reagan's victory in the electoral college was even more stunning: 489 votes to Carter's 49.

CARTER'S FINAL MONTHS AS PRESIDENT

Although devastated by the election results, Carter was determined not to waste a moment of the two and a half months left to him as president. In December, he pushed two important pieces of environmental legislation through Congress: the "Superfund" Bill and the Alaska National Interest Lands Conservation Act. The first bill established a $1.6 billion "superfund" for the clean up of toxic chemicals accidentally released—or surreptitiously dumped—into the environment by industry. The second bill placed more than 100 million acres of Alaskan wilderness under the protection of the federal government.

The determination with which Carter battled for the passage of these two bills, even after losing the election, testifies to his profound commitment to preserving the environment. Indeed, Carter has been described as the greatest environmental president after Theodore Roosevelt.

During his presidency, he opposed wasteful "pork-barrel" water projects, signed into law clean water and air acts rejected by earlier administrations, added to the endangered species list, and protected fragile wetlands and desert environments. Most significantly, he doubled the total area of U.S. wildlife refuges and national parks with the Alaska

President Carter's Farewell Address

The following are excerpts from President Carter's Farewell Address delivered on January 14, 1981, a week before he left office:

For a few minutes now, I want to lay aside my role as leader of our nation, and speak to you as a fellow citizen of the world about three difficult issues: The threat of nuclear destruction, our stewardship of the physical resources of our planet, and the pre-eminence of the basic rights of human beings.

It's now been 35 years since the first atomic bomb fell on Hiroshima. The great majority of the world's people cannot remember a time when the nuclear shadow did not hang over the earth. Our minds have adjusted to it, as after a time our eyes adjust to the dark.

Yet the risk of nuclear conflagration has not lessened. . . .

The danger is becoming greater. As the arsenals of the superpowers grow in size and sophistication and as other governments acquire these weapons, it may only be a matter of time before madness, desperation, greed or miscalculation lets lose this terrible force . . .

Nuclear weapons are an expression of one side of our human character. But there is another side. The same rocket technology

A Crisis of Confidence: 1979–1981

Lands Act, legislation he doggedly fought for against the powerful oil, mineral, and timber interests that sought to exploit the Alaskan wilderness.

During his final months in office, Carter also continued to labor tirelessly for the release of the 52 American hostages still in Iran. Assisted by the Algerian government,

> that delivers nuclear warheads has also taken us peacefully into space. From that perspective, we see our Earth as it really is—a small and fragile and beautiful blue globe, the only home we have. We see no barriers of race or religion or country. We see the essential unity of our species and our planet . . .
>
> Another major challenge, therefore, is to protect the quality of this world within which we live. The shadows that fall across the future are cast not only by the kinds of weapons we have built, but by the kind of world we will either nourish or neglect . . .
>
> I have just been talking about forces of potential destruction that mankind has developed, and how we might control them. It is equally important that we remember the beneficial forces that we have evolved over the ages, and how to hold fast to them.
>
> One of those constructive forces is enhancement of individual human freedoms through the strengthening of democracy, and the fight against deprivation, torture, terrorism and the persecution of people throughout the world. The struggle for human rights overrides all differences of color, nation or language . . . .
>
> I believe with all my heart that America must always stand for these basic human rights—at home and abroad. That is both our history and our destiny . . .

Carter spent the last months of his presidency working for the release of the 52 hostages in Iran; in fact, he spent the last 48 hours of his time as president on the phone arranging the transfer of Iranian funds that had been frozen. With the help of the Algerian government working as an intermediary, Carter arranged the release, which happened on Ronald Reagan's inauguration day. Although he was no longer president, Carter flew to West Germany to watch as the hostages got off the planes from Iran.

which volunteered to act as an intermediary between Tehran and Washington, the president struck a deal with the Iranians. He agreed to release $3 billion of the $13 billion in frozen Iranian assets still in American banks in return for the hostages' freedom. During the last

A Crisis of Confidence: 1979–1981

48 hours of his presidency, Carter was on the telephone almost continuously, monitoring the final arrangements for the transfer of the frozen Iranian gold and cash, a complex process involving an army of bankers, accountants, lawyers, and diplomats.

After numerous delays by the Iranians, a final agreement was signed in Algeria on the morning of January 20, 1981—Ronald Reagan' inauguration day. The hostages were boarded onto two airplanes, but Iranian authorities postponed their take off until after Reagan's swearing-in. Despite the Iranians' cruel insistence that the hostages not be released until after he had left office, Carter was elated. The Americans' 444-day ordeal was finally over and every one of them was alive. That evening, at Reagan's suggestion, Carter flew to West Germany to personally welcome the 52 men and women he had worked so long to free. Then, the exhausted ex-president returned home to Plains to begin what he regarded as "an altogether new, unwanted, and potentially empty life."

6

"CITIZEN OF A TROUBLED WORLD": 1981 AND BEYOND

SOON AFTER LOSING the election, Carter received more bad news. His Plains warehouse business, which had been administered by a blind trust over the last four years, was heavily in debt. Carter, however, refused to resort to the lecture tour or to sitting on corporate boards—two lucrative and readily available options for former presidents. Instead, he and Rosalynn decided to sell the warehouse and use the proceeds from their memoirs and other books they wrote to save the family farm. Over the years, Carter would author more than a dozen books on a variety of subjects, from his boyhood in Georgia to the war-torn Middle East. He even published a collection of original poems.

CITIZEN OF A TROUBLED WORLD: 1981 AND BEYOND

The Carters became active in Habitat for Humanity, an organization that builds and refurbishes apartments and houses for low-income families, after Jimmy Carter left the presidency. They also founded the Carter Presidential Center, associated with Emory University in Atlanta.

During his first years out of office, Carter was almost completely disregarded by the public, the press, and even his own political party. His monumental environmental legislation, his crucial role in attaining Israeli-Egyptian peace, and his far-sighted attempts to reduce the country's dependency on foreign oil seemed all but forgotten. Instead, commentators tended to focus on the negative aspects of the Carter years: inflation, the hostage crisis, and "malaise." The former president, as journalist Meg Greenfield sadly noted, was enduring an "unfair fate" as a "shunned figure" and "no one seems willing . . . to give him a break or bit of dignity or anything."

Yet Carter refused to give in to bitterness or despair. Soon after his defeat at the polls, he received a heartening letter from his former naval commander, Admiral Hyman Rickover. "As long as a man is trying as hard as he can to do what he thinks to be right, he is a success regardless of outcome," Rickover wrote. Convinced he had indeed done his best to meet the pressing domestic and international challenges of his presidency, Carter decided to devote himself to continuing the work that had been closest to his heart as chief executive: promoting human rights and world peace.

THE CARTER PRESIDENTIAL CENTER
In January 1982, Carter, who had spent much of the past year planning his presidential library, had an exciting idea. Instead of simply establishing an archive for his papers, he would combine his library with a public policy institute. And his new presidential center would not only be a "think tank" where scholars analyzed issues such as international conflict resolution, it would also be an activist organization whose staff would travel around the globe to advance human rights and fight poverty. Carter's partner in this undertaking would be his wife Rosalynn, one of his closest advisors from the beginning of his political career. Rosalynn had been an exceptionally active first lady, representing Carter on a diplomatic tour of Latin America, chairing a presidential commission on mental health,

and even listening in on cabinet meetings. Not surprisingly, she became an enthusiastic partner in her husband's newest endeavor.

PRESIDENT CARTER'S LEGACY
The Carter Center

Most historians view Jimmy Carter's role as mediator during the Egyptian-Israeli Peace Treaty negotiations as his most significant accomplishment. Many people, however, including Carter himself, consider the Carter Presidential Center to be the 39th president's most important legacy. When Jimmy and Rosalynn Carter first created their nonprofit public policy institute in 1982, the center employed a handful of employees. Today, the center, which adjoins the Jimmy Carter Library and Museum, employs some 200 men and women, including field representatives in South America and Africa. Many volunteers also donate their time and expertise to the institution.

Devoted to alleviating human suffering around the world, Jimmy Carter and the center's staff have participated in peace negotiations in such diverse places as Bosnia and Sudan. They have monitored critical elections in emerging democracies on several continents and have labored to eradicate devastating diseases and teach modern agricultural techniques in a host of Third World nations. Through the center's numerous programs, the former president continues to promote human rights and racial, ethnic, and religious tolerance around the world.

The Carter Center is a testament not only to Carter's profound commitment to live his Christian beliefs by helping others, but also to the former president's perseverance and resiliency. As his biographer Douglas Brinkley has noted, despite his crushing electoral defeat in 1980, Carter refused to give up on the policies and ideals he most believed in as president, particularly the advancement of human rights and international peace. Through the Carter Center, Jimmy Carter has created a legacy of humanitarianism, democracy, and peacemaking that he hopes will last long beyond his own lifetime.

As the Carters formulated plans for their new center, which was to be affiliated with Atlanta's Emory University, they also took the time to assist a variety of charitable causes. Foremost among these was Habitat for Humanity, a nonprofit organization devoted to building homes for the poor. In September 1984, Rosalynn and Jimmy boarded a bus for New York City with other Habitat for Humanity volunteers from Georgia to spend the next week refurbishing a rundown apartment building. When the media discovered what the Carters were up to, reporters were entranced by the sight of a former president and first lady nailing Sheetrock and laying floors for 10 hours a day in one of New York's poorest neighborhoods. Americans began to feel a new affection for the man they had so thoroughly rejected at the polls four years earlier.

In October 1986, Carter's standing with the public and press received another boost when President Reagan traveled to Atlanta to speak at the opening ceremonies for the Carter Presidential Center (as the Carter Center and presidential library are collectively known) and enthusiastically praised his former rival. "You gave yourself to your country, gracing the White House with your passion and intellect and commitment," Reagan declared. "Your countrymen have vivid memories of your time in the White House still. They see you working in the Oval Office at your desk with an air of intense concentration; repairing to a quiet place to receive the latest word on the hostages you did so much to free; or studying in your hideaway office for the meeting at Camp David that would mark such a breakthrough for peace in the Middle East." At last, Carter was being afforded that "bit of dignity" that journalist Meg Greenfield believed he had been so unjustly denied when he first left the White House.

CARTER'S REMARKABLE POST-PRESIDENCY

Over the years since its founding, the Carter Center has supported peace and democracy and has eased human suffering in more than 60 countries around the globe. Some of the Center's greatest accomplishments have been in the area of health. Carter and his staff have led efforts to immunize children in Third World countries against dangerous viruses and to fight guinea worm disease, a horrific illness linked to contaminated drinking water.

In 1989, a new project was initiated through the Carter Presidential Center as the former president started monitoring elections in developing democracies. That year he oversaw elections in Panama, where he boldly took on military dictator Manuel Noriega for manipulating the voting in favor of his handpicked successor. The following year, Carter helped monitor elections in another Central American country, Nicaragua. Using his prestige as a former U.S. president, he pressured the defeated military strongman Daniel Ortega to peacefully relinquish power to president-elect Violeta Chamarro. Since 1990, Carter has observed elections in a host of other emerging democracies, including the Dominican Republic, Guyana, Liberia, and Jamaica.

During the 1990s, Carter gained international praise

for his numerous peacemaking missions to strife-ridden regions around the globe. Carter was particularly influential in mediating international disputes during Democratic President Bill Clinton's first term in office. In 1994, Carter's

"With Words We Learn to Hate"

Carter's deep commitment to promoting peace and understanding among the various nations and peoples of the world is evident in this poem from his volume, *Always a Reckoning*.

"With Words We Learn to Hate"

We take lives in times of peace
for crimes we won't forgive,
claiming some have forfeited
the right to live.

We justify our nation's wars
each time with words to prove we kill
in a moral cause.

We've cursed the names of those we fought—
the "Japs" instead of Japanese,
German Nazis or the "Huns,"
and "Wops"—when they were enemies.

Later, they became our friends,
but habits live in memories.

So now, when others disagree
we hate again, and with our might,
war by war, name by dirty name,
prove we're right.

CITIZEN OF A TROUBLED WORLD: 1981 AND BEYOND

Jimmy Carter has slowed down the fast pace he kept as president, but he still makes trips to promote peace. In May 2002, he and Rosalynn traveled to Cuba to meet with Communist ruler Fidel Castro (center). Carter called for the United States to end travel and trade restrictions with Cuba and for Castro to end human rights abuses and to institute free elections.

negotiations with North Korean leader Kim Il Sung did much to defuse the tensions between the United States and North Korea over North Korea's expanding nuclear weapons program. Later that same year, Carter helped avert a U.S. military invasion of Haiti when he and an American mediation team persuaded military dictator Raoul Cedras to step down in favor of the popularly-elected president, Jean-Bertrand Aristide.

Now in his late seventies, Carter has slowed his pace, spending more of his time in Plains, where he and Rosalynn still live in the house they built more than four decades ago.

But Carter has not abandoned his mission to promote international peace and human rights, by any means. In May 2002, he made a historic trip to Cuba to meet with its Communist ruler, Fidel Castro, who has been shunned by the U.S. government since seizing power in 1959. In Cuba, Carter publicly called for the United States to end travel and trade restrictions with the island and for Castro to halt his human rights abuses and institute free elections.

The Nobel Peace Prize

The following excerpts are from Jimmy Carter's acceptance speech for the Nobel Peace Prize, December 2002, at Oslo, Norway:

I thought often during my years in the White House of an admonition that we received in our small school in Plains, Georgia, from a beloved teacher, Miss Julia Coleman. She often said, 'We must adjust to changing times and still hold to unchanging principles.'

I am not here as a public official, but as a citizen of a troubled world who finds hope in a growing consensus that the generally accepted goals of society are peace, freedom, human rights, environmental quality, the alleviation of suffering, and the rule of law . . . .

War may sometimes be a necessary evil. But no matter how necessary, it is always an evil, never a good. We will not learn how to live together in peace by killing each other's children.

The bond of our common humanity is stronger than the divisiveness of our fears and prejudices. God gives us the capacity for choice. We can choose to alleviate suffering. We can choose to work together for peace. We can make changes—and we must.

Citizen of a Troubled World: 1981 and Beyond

In January 2003, Carter traveled to the troubled South American nation of Venezuela to try to mediate an economically devastating general strike called by President Hugo Chavez's political opponents.

Over the course of his remarkable post-presidency, Carter has been honored with numerous awards, including the 1999 Presidential Medal of Freedom. When he was awarded the Nobel Peace Prize three years later in 2002, Carter used his acceptance speech to speak out strongly in support of nonviolent resolutions to international conflicts. As he approaches the eighth decade of his life, Jimmy Carter is as committed as ever to making the world a more peaceful and compassionate place.

THE PRESIDENTS OF THE UNITED STATES

George Washington
1789–1797

John Adams
1797–1801

Thomas Jefferson
1801–1809

James Madison
1809–1817

James Monroe
1817–1825

John Quincy Adams
1825–1829

Andrew Jackson
1829–1837

Martin Van Buren
1837–1841

William Henry Harrison
1841

John Tyler
1841–1845

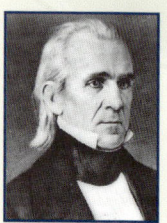

James Polk
1845–1849

Zachary Taylor
1849–1850

Millard Filmore
1850–1853

Franklin Pierce
1853–1857

James Buchanan
1857–1861

Abraham Lincoln
1861–1865

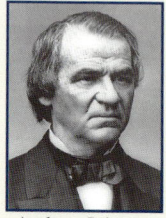

Andrew Johnson
1865–1869

Ulysses S. Grant
1869–1877

Rutherford B. Hayes
1877–1881

James Garfield
1881

Chester Arthur 1881–1885	 Grover Cleveland 1885–1889	 Benjamin Harrison 1889–1893	 Grover Cleveland 1893–1897	 William McKinley 1897–1901
 Theodore Roosevelt 1901–1909	 William H. Taft 1909–1913	 Woodrow Wilson 1913–1921	 Warren Harding 1921–1923	 Calvin Coolidge 1923–1929
 Herbert Hoover 1929–1933	 Franklin D. Roosevelt 1933–1945	 Harry S. Truman 1945–1953	 Dwight Eisenhower 1953–1961	 John F. Kennedy 1961–1963
 Lyndon Johnson 1963–1969	 Richard Nixon 1969–1974	 Gerald Ford 1974–1977	 Jimmy Carter 1977–1981	 Ronald Reagan 1981–1989
 George H.W. Bush 1989–1993	 William J. Clinton 1993–2001	 George W. Bush 2001–		

Note: Dates indicate years of presidential service.
Source: www.whitehouse.gov

Presidential Fact File

THE CONSTITUTION

Article II of the Constitution of the United States outlines several requirements for the president of the United States, including:

- ★ **Age:** The president must be at least 35 years old.
- ★ **Citizenship:** The president must be a U.S. citizen.
- ★ **Residency:** The president must have lived in the United States for at least 14 years.
- ★ **Oath of Office:** On his inauguration, the president takes this oath: "I do solemnly swear (or affirm) that I will faithfully execute the office of President of the United States, and will to the best of my ability, preserve, protect and defend the Constitution of the United States."
- ★ **Term:** A presidential term lasts four years.

PRESIDENTIAL POWERS

The president has many distinct powers as outlined in and interpreted from the Constitution. The president:

- ★ Submits many proposals to Congress for regulatory, social, and economic reforms.
- ★ Appoints federal judges with the Senate's approval.
- ★ Prepares treaties with foreign nations to be approved by the Senate.
- ★ Can veto laws passed by Congress.
- ★ Acts as commander in chief of the military to oversee military strategy and actions.
- ★ Appoints members of the cabinet and many other agencies and administrations with the Senate's approval.
- ★ Can declare martial law (control of local governments within the country) in times of national crisis.

Presidential Fact File

TRADITION

Many parts of the presidency developed out of tradition. The traditions listed below are but a few that are associated with the U.S. presidency.

★ After taking his oath of office, George Washington added, "So help me God." Numerous presidents since Washington have also added this phrase to their oath.

★ Originally, the Constitution limited the term of the presidency to four years, but did not limit the number of terms a president could serve. Presidents, following the precedent set by George Washington, traditionally served only two terms. After Franklin Roosevelt was elected to four terms, however, Congress amended the Constitution to restrict presidents to only two.

★ James Monroe was the first president to have his inauguration outside the Capitol. From his inauguration in 1817 to Jimmy Carter's inauguration in 1977, it was held on the Capitol's east portico. Ronald Reagan broke from this tradition in 1981 when he was inaugurated on the west portico to face his home state, California. Since 1981, all presidential inaugurations have been held on the west portico of the Capitol.

★ Not all presidential traditions are serious, however. One of the more fun activities connected with the presidency began when President William Howard Taft ceremoniously threw out the first pitch of the new baseball season in 1910. Presidents since Taft have carried on this tradition, including Woodrow Wilson, who is pictured here as he throws the first pitch of the 1916 season. In more recent years, the president has also opened the All-Star and World Series games.

Presidential Fact File

THE WHITE HOUSE

Although George Washington was involved with the planning of the White House, he never lived there. It has been, however, the official residence of every president beginning with John Adams, the second U.S. president. The building was completed approximately in 1800, although it has undergone several renovations since then. It was the first public building constructed in Washington, D.C. The White House has 132 rooms, several of which are open to the public. Private rooms include those for administration and the president's personal residence. For an online tour of the White House and other interesting facts, visit the official White House website, *http://www.whitehouse.gov*.

THE PRESIDENTIAL SEAL

A committee began planning the presidential seal in 1777. It was completed in 1782. The seal appears as an official stamp on medals, stationery, and documents, among other items. Originally, the eagle faced right toward the arrows (a symbol of war) that it held in its talons. In 1945, President Truman had the seal altered so that the eagle's head instead faced left toward the olive branch (a symbol of peace), because he believed the president should be prepared for war but always look toward peace.

President Carter in Profile

PERSONAL

Name: James Earl Carter, Jr.

Birth date: October 1, 1924

Birth place: Plains, Georgia

Father: James Earl Carter

Mother: Lillian Gordy Carter

Wife: Eleanor Rosalynn Smith

Children: John William "Jack" Carter, James Earl "Chip" Carter, Donnel Jeffrey "Jeff" Carter, Amy Lynn Carter

POLITICAL

Years in office: 1977–1981

Vice president: Walter Mondale

Occupations before presidency: Farmer, public official

Political party: Democrat

Major achievements of presidency: The "Superfund" Bill, the Alaska National Interest Lands Conservation Act, the freeing of 52 American hostages in Iran, and the Egyptian-Israeli Peace Treaty

Presidential library:

The Jimmy Carter Library and Museum
441 Freedom Parkway
Atlanta, GA 30307
404-331-3942
http://www.jimmycarterlibrary.org

Tributes:

The Jimmy Carter National Historic Site
   (Plains, GA; http://www.nps.gov/jica/)

The Carter Center
   (Atlanta, GA; http://www.cartercenter.org/)

Chronology

1924	James Earl (Jimmy) Carter, Jr., is born in Plains, Georgia, on October 1
1943–1946	Attends U.S. Naval Academy at Annapolis, Maryland
1946	Marries Rosalynn Smith shortly after graduation from the Naval Academy
1952	Chosen by Admiral Rickover to participate in nuclear submarine project
1953	Resigns from Navy to take over family farm and peanut warehouse business in Plains following his father's death
1963–1967	Serves as Democratic member of Georgia state senate
1966	Runs unsuccessfully for governor of Georgia
1970	Elected governor of Georgia
1973–74	Watergate scandal leads to resignation of President Nixon August 1974; Vice President Gerald Ford becomes president
1974	Carter announces candidacy for president
1976	
July	Wins Democratic Party nomination
November	Wins presidential election by slim margin against Gerald Ford
1977	
January	Inaugurated 39th president of United States
April	Proposes comprehensive energy program
1978	
April	Panama Canal treaties ratified by Senate
September	Carter brokers talks at Camp David between Egyptian President Anwar el-Sadat and Israeli Prime Minister Menachem Begin resulting in Camp David Accords
1979	
January	Diplomatic relations with People's Republic of China are normalized

Chronology

March 26	Egyptian-Israeli Peace Treaty signed in Washington, D.C.
June	SALT II Treaty between the United States and the Soviet Union signed
July	Carter delivers so-called "Malaise Speech"
November	Iranian militants take U.S. citizens hostage in Tehran
December	Soviet troops invade Afghanistan
1980	The United States announces sanctions against the Soviet Union in response to Afghanistan invasion
April	Hostage rescue mission fails
August	Carter receives Democratic presidential nomination at national convention
November	Loses presidential election to Ronald Reagan by a landslide
December	Signs Alaska Lands Bill and "Superfund" Bill
1981	52 American hostages released by Iranian militants as Reagan is being inaugurated on January 20
1982	Planning for the Carter Center begins
1989	Carter monitors elections in Panama
1990	Monitors elections in Nicaragua
1994	Meets with Kim Il Sung regarding North Korea's nuclear weapons program. Helps negotiate a peaceful transfer of political power in Haiti
2002	
May	Travels to Cuba and meets with Fidel Castro
October	Awarded Nobel Peace Prize
2003	Attempts to negotiate an end to the general strike in Venezuela

Bibliography

Bourne, Peter G. *Jimmy Carter: A Comprehensive Biography from Plains to Post-presidency*. New York: Scribner's, 1997.

Brzezinski, Zbigniew, and Stuart E. Eizenstat. "Carter's Winning Presidency," *The Washington Post*, October 22, 2002.

Brinkley, Douglas. *The Unfinished Presidency: Jimmy Carter's Journey Beyond the White House*. New York: Viking, 1998.

Carter, Jimmy. *Always a Reckoning, and Other Poems*. New York: Random House, 1995.

———. *An Hour before Daylight: Memories of a Rural Boyhood*. New York: Simon & Schuster, 2001.

———. *Keeping Faith: Memoirs of a President*. New York: Bantam Books, 1982.

———. *Living Faith*. New York: Times Books, 1996.

———. *Why Not the Best?* Nashville: Broadman Press, 1975.

Carter, Rosalynn. *First Lady from Plains*. Boston: Houghton Mifflin, 1984.

Fink, Gary M., and Hugh Davis Graham, eds. *The Carter Presidency: Policy Choices in the Post-New Deal Era*. Lawrence, Kan.: University Press of Kansas, 1998.

Graff, Henry F., ed. *The Presidents: A Reference History*. New York: Charles Scribners' Sons, 1996.

"Jimmy Carter: American Experience" (Transcripts of PBS television program) *http://www.pbs.org/wgbh/amex/carter*

Morris, Kenneth E. *Jimmy Carter: American Moralist*. Athens, Ga.: University of Georgia Press, 1996.

Further Reading

Acker, Kerry. *Jimmy Carter.* Philadelphia: Chelsea House, 2002.

Carter, Jimmy. *An Hour before Daylight: Memories of a Rural Boyhood.* New York: Simon & Schuster, 2001.

———. *Talking Peace: A Vision for the Next Generation.* New York: Dutton Children's Books, 1995.

———. *Why Not the Best?* Nashville: Broadman Press, 1975.

Carter, Rosalynn. *First Lady from Plains.* Boston: Houghton Mifflin, 1984.

Slavin, Ed. *Jimmy Carter.* Philadelphia: Chelsea House, 1989.

WEBSITES

The Carter Center
http://www.cartercenter.org

Habitat for Humanity: Jimmy Carter and Habitat
http://www.habitat.org/how/carter.html

Jimmy Carter Library
http://carterlibrary.galileo.peachnet.edu/

Jimmy Carter: American Experience
http://www.pbs.org/wgbh/amex/carter

INDEX

Adams, John
 and the revolution against the British, 7
 as U.S. president, 96
Adams, John Quincy, 12
Afghanistan
 Soviet invasion of, 14, 74, 99
Agnew, Spiro, 42
Alaska National Interest Lands Conservation Act, 77–79, 97, 99
Al-Gadhafi, Mu'ammar, 75
Algeria
 assistance with the hostage crisis, 79–81
Always a Reckoning and Other Poems (Carter), 21, 88
Anderson, John
 and the presidential election of 1980, 77
Annapolis, Maryland, 26, 98
American Revolution, 7
Archery, Georgia
 Carter family move to, 17–19
 segregation in, 23–24
Aristide, Jean-Bertrand, 89
Atlanta, Georgia, 12, 14, 26, 38, 83, 86

Begin, Menachem,
 Israeli prime minister, 98
 and the Nobel peace prize, 63–65
 and peace treaty with Egypt, 63–65

Brezhnev, Leonid,
 Russian president, 62
Brinkley, Douglas
 Carter biographer, 85
Brzezinski, Zbigniew
 Carter's national security advisor, 61
Bush, George W.
 as war president, 8
Byrd, Robert
 majority leader, 56

Califano, Joseph
 Carter's secretary of health, education and welfare, 52
Camp David Accords, 69, 86
 Carter's role in, 12–13, 63–65, 98
Carter, Amy Lynn (daughter), 33, 97
Carter, Billy (brother), 25, 30
 financial dealings of, 75
Carter, Donnel "Jeff" Jeffrey (son), 30, 33, 97
Carter, Eleanor Rosalynn Smith (wife), 12, 14, 30, 82, 85–86, 89, 97
 as first lady, 84
 marriage of, 27–28, 98
Carter, Gloria (sister), 16–17, 25, 30
Carter, James Earl (father), 26, 97
 ambitions of, 16–21
 and civil rights, 24, 29
 generosity of, 30
 death of, 29–30, 33, 98

Carter, James "Jimmy" Earl Jr.
 accomplishments of, 15, 66–67, 77–79, 83, 87
 Always a Reckoning and Other Poems, 21, 88
 as author, 82
 birth of, 16–17, 97–98
 cabinet of, 52
 and the Camp David Accords, 12–13, 98
 childhood of, 18–20
 conflicts with Congress, 51–58, 62, 66
 criticism of, 14, 46–47, 65–69, 71–73, 75–76, 83
 education of, 25–26
 on education, 34, 66
 energy program of, 51, 53–56, 98
 environmental legislation of, 77–79, 83, 90
 farewell address of, 78–79
 as farmer, 97–98
 foreign policy issues of, 57–63, 72–74
 as Georgia governor, 15, 36–40, 45, 98
 and Georgia state senate, 34–35, 98
 "good mental health habits" of, 24
 and the hostage crisis, 14, 72–73, 75–77, 79–81, 83, 86, 97, 99
 and human rights, 12–13, 59–61, 63, 84–85, 89–91

102

INDEX

"I Wanted to Share My Father's World", 21
inaugural speech of, 50
international peacemaker, 11–14, 62–65, 83–85, 87–91
and the Iranian hostage crisis, 14
marriage of, 27–28, 98
monitoring of foreign elections, 12–14, 85, 87, 89, 90, 99
and the Nobel Peace Prize, 10–13, 63, 90–91, 99
"people's president," 48–439
poetry of, 21
and politics, 15, 32–71, 97
post-presidential contributions of, 12–13, 82–91
and presidential election of 1976, 40–42, 44–47, 98
and presidential election of 1980, 74–77, 99
and Presidential Medal of Freedom, 91
on racial and gender discrimination, 38–39, 52
and segregation, 22–23, 32–34
spiritual conversion of, 36, 85
and treaties, 58–59, 62–65

and the U.S. Navy, 26–30, 43, 98
as U.S. president, 10–12, 15, 20, 47–80, 89, 95, 97–98
Why Not the Best?, 43
"With Words We Learn to Hate," 88
Carter, James "Chip" Earl (son), 30, 33, 97
Carter, John "Jack" William (son), 30, 33, 97
Carter, Lillian Gordy (mother), 30, 97
and civil rights, 24–25
as nurse, 18, 24–25
Carter, Ruth (sister), 25, 27–28, 30
as Christian evangelist, 36
"Carter Doctrine" protection of the Persian Gulf in, 74
Carter Presidential Center, 97
international peace and human rights and, 12–14, 85, 87
opening of, 86–87
planning for, 83–87, 99
Castro, Fidel, 89, 99
Cedras, Raoul, 89
Chamarro, Violeta, 87
Chavez, Hugo, 91
China, People's Republic of, 60–61, 98
Civil Rights Act of 1964, 37
Civil Rights Movement, 24, 32, 60
Clinton, Bill
as U.S. president, 88
Cold War, 61

Coleman, Julia
Carter's high school principal, 25, 90
Cronkite, Walter
foreword, 6–9
Cuba, 89, 99

Democratic Political Party, 15, 34–35, 41–42, 44, 51–52, 88, 97–99
National Convention of 1972, 41
National Convention of 1976, 44–45
National Convention of 1980, 75
Department of Education establishment of, 66

Egypt
peace agreements with Israel, 12–13, 62–65, 83
Egyptian-Israeli Peace Treaty (1979), 12, 63–65, 83, 85, 97, 99
El-Sadat, Anwar, Egyptian president, 98
and the Nobel peace prize, 63–64
and peace treaty with Israel, 63–65
Emory University, 83, 86
Energy program, 51, 53–56, 98
England
and the American Revolution, 7

Ford, Gerald,
criticism of, 46–47
as president, 42, 44–46, 52, 57, 61, 98
and presidential election of 1976, 44–47, 98

103

INDEX

Georgia, 37, 86
  racial problems in, 35
  state senate, 34–35, 39, 98
Georgia Institute of Technology, 26
Gordy, Tom (uncle), 26
Great Depression, 19
Greenfield, Meg
  on Carter, 83, 87

Habitat for Humanity
  and the Carters, 83, 86
Haiti
  transfer of political power in, 12, 89, 99
Hoover, Herbert, 12
Hurst, Joe, 35
Hussein, Saddam, Iraqi dictator, 76

"I Wanted to Share My Father's World" (Carter)
  relationship with father in, 21
Iran, 60, 71, 76
  anti-American protests in, 72
  Muslim fundamentalists in, 68
  and the U.S. embassy hostages, 72–73, 76–77, 79–81, 83, 86, 99
Iranian hostage crisis
  and Carter, 14, 72–73, 75–77, 79–81, 83, 86, 97, 99
  failed rescue attempt, 73, 99
Israel
  peace agreements with Egypt, 12–13, 62–65, 83
  and the Yom Kippur Wars, 53, 64

Japan
  bombing of Pearl Harbor, 26
Jefferson, Thomas
  and the Louisiana Purchase, 7
  and the revolution against the British, 7
Jimmy Carter Library and Museum, 84–85, 97
Jimmy Carter National Historic Site, 97
Johnson, Leroy
  Georgia state senator, 39
Johnson, Lyndon
  as president, 57
Jordan, Hamilton
  Carter's aide, 37, 41, 52

Kennedy, Edward (Senator), 51
  and the presidential election of 1980, 74–75
Khomeini, Ayatollah, 71–72
  death of, 76
Kreps, Juanita
  as secretary of commerce, 52

Lance, Bert
  accusations of financial misdealing, 67–68
Lincoln, Abraham
  as wartime president, 7
Louisiana Purchase, 7–8

Maddox, Lester, 35
  as governor of Georgia, 36–37

Madison, James
  and the revolution against the British, 7
"Malaise Speech", 70–71, 83, 99
McGovern, George (Senator), 41
Mondale, Walter
  Carter's vice president, 44–45, 57, 97
Monroe, James
  as U.S. president, 95

Nicaragua
  elections in, 87, 99
Niebuhr, Reinhold
  Christian ideals of, 36
Nixon, Richard
  pardoning of, 46
  as president of, 41–42, 54, 57, 61
  resignation of, 42, 98
  and Watergate scandal, 41–42, 98
Nobel Peace Prize
  and Begin, 63
  and Carter, 10–13, 63, 90–91, 99
  and el-Sadat, 63
  and Roosevelt, T., 10–11
  and Wilson, 10–11
Norfolk, Virginia, 27–28
Noriega, Manuel, 87
North Korea
  nuclear weapons program of, 89, 99
Nuclear submarine project
  and Admiral Rickover, 29, 43, 98

Office of Management and Budget, 67–68

104

INDEX

O'Neill, Thomas "Tip" P., Speaker of the House, 51
  support of Carter's energy program, 55
Organization of Petroleum Exporting Countries (OPEC), 68
Ortega, Daniel, 87
Oslo, Norway, 10–11, 90

Panama, 57
  elections in, 87, 99
  treaties with, 57–59, 98
Panama Canal treaties, 57–59, 62, 75, 98
"Peanut Brigade," 44
Pearl Harbor, Hawaii
  Japanese bombing of, 26
Plains, Georgia, 44, 90
  Carter's birthplace, 10, 16–18, 97–98
  Carters' return to, 30–33, 81–82, 89
  racial turmoil in, 32
  segregation in, 24, 32–33
Plains High School, 25
Playboy
  Carter's interview in, 46–47
Powell, Jody
  Carter's aide, 37, 41
  Carter's press secretary, 52
Presidential election of 1976, 40–42, 44–47, 98
Presidential election of 1980, 74–77, 99
Presidential Medal of Freedom, 91

Presidents of the United States, 92–96
  and the constitution, 94
  fact file of, 94–96
  powers of, 8, 94
  and the Presidential Seal, 96
  and tradition, 95
  and the White House, 12–13, 15, 47–48, 63, 73, 86–87, 90, 96

Reagan, Ronald, 57
  as California's governor, 45, 75
  inauguration of, 80–81
  and presidential election of 1980, 74–77, 99
  speech at the Carter Center, 86
Republican Political Party, 35, 45–46
Rickover, Admiral Hyman, 98
  creator of nuclear submarine program, 29, 43
  influence on Carter, 29, 84
Roosevelt, Franklin Delano
  "new deal" of, 76
  as wartime president, 7
Roosevelt, Theodore, 57
  environmental president, 77
  and the Nobel Peace Prize, 10–11

Sakharov, Andrei
  Russian dissident, 61–62

SALT II Treaty (Strategic Arms Limitations Talks)
  withdrawal of, 74
  United States and Soviet Union, 61–62, 99
Sanders, Carl
  as Georgia's governor, 37–38
Segregation
  in the south, 22–25, 32–37
Six Day War (1967), 64
"Superfund" Bill, 77, 97, 99
Soviet Union, 47, 59, 61
  invasion of Afghanistan, 14, 74, 99
  treaties with, 61–62, 99
  U.S. sanctions against, 74, 99
Sung, Kim Il, North Korean leader, 89, 99

Three Mile Island
  accident at, 69
Time (magazine)
  Carter on the cover, 39–40
Torrijos, Omar
  and Panama Canal treaty, 59
Truman, Harry S.
  as U.S. president, 8, 96

United Nations, 52
United States of America
  boycott of Olympic games, 74
  economic problems of, 68, 71, 75–76
  fuel shortage of, 53–54, 68–71

105

INDEX

government branches
  of, 9
sanctions against
  Soviet Union, 74, 99
treaties and, 98–99
and wartime, 8, 26
United States Congress,
  8, 76, 94–95
  Carter's conflicts with,
    51–58, 62, 66
United States Constitution, 8–9
  and presidency
    requirements, 7,
    94–95
United States Naval
  Academy
  Carter's training at,
    26–29, 43, 98
United States Supreme
  Court
  ruling on segregation
    in public schools,
    32

U.S.S. *Sea Wolf*
  Carter officer on,
    28–29

Vance, Cyrus
  Carter's secretary of
    state, 52, 61, 73
Venezuela
  general strike in, 12,
    91, 99
Vietnam War, 57–58, 69
Vinson, Fred, 8

Wallace, George
  governor of Alabama,
    37–38
Washington, D.C., 41
  as U.S. capital, 49, 96, 98
Washington, George
  and the revolution
    against the British,
    7
  as U.S. president,
    95–96

Watergate scandal, 98
  Nixon's role in, 41–42,
    44
White Citizens Council,
  32–33
Why Not the Best? (Carter)
  Carter's autobiography,
    43
"Why Not the Best?"
  presidential campaign
    slogan, 29
Wilson, Woodrow
  and the Nobel Peace
    Prize, 10–11
  as wartime president, 7
"With Words We Learn
  to Hate" (Carter), 88
World War II, 26–27

Yom Kippur Wars,
  53–54, 64
Young, Andrew
  as ambassador to the
    United Nations, 52

Picture Credits

page:

11:	© Associated Press, POOL	59:	Courtesy of Jimmy Carter Library
14:	Courtesy of Emma Seimodei	64:	© Bettmann/CORBIS
17:	Courtesy of Jimmy Carter Library	67:	© Bettmann/CORBIS
22:	Courtesy of Jimmy Carter Library	72:	© Associated Press, AP
28:	Courtesy of Jimmy Carter Library	80:	Courtesy of Jimmy Carter Library
33:	© Bettmann/CORBIS	83:	© Associated Press, AP
40:	© Time Inc./Time Life Pictures/ Getty Images	89:	© Associated Press, AP
45:	© Bettmann/CORBIS	92-93:	Courtesy Library of Congress, "Portraits of the Presidents and First Ladies" American Memory Collection
49:	Courtesy of Jimmy Carter Library		
55:	Courtesy of Jimmy Carter Library		

Cover: Library of Congress, LC-USZC4-599

Acknowledgments

Thank you to Celebrity Speakers Intl. for coordinating Mr. Cronkite's contribution to this book.

About the Contributors

Louise Chipley Slavicek received her master's degree in history from the University of Connecticut. She has written many articles on historical topics for young people's magazines and is the author of seven other books for young people, including *Women of the Revolutionary War*, *Israel*, and *Juan Ponce de León*. She lives in Ohio with her husband Jim, a research biologist, and their two children, Krista and Nathan.

Walter Cronkite has covered virtually every major news event during his more than 60 years in journalism, during which he earned a reputation for being "the most trusted man in America." He began his career as a reporter for the United Press during World War II, taking part in the beachhead assaults of Normandy and covering the Nuremberg trials. He then joined *CBS News* in Washington, D.C., where he was the news anchor for political convention and election coverage from 1952 to 1980. CBS debuted its first half-hour weeknight news program with Mr. Cronkite's interview of President John F. Kennedy in 1963. Mr. Cronkite was inducted into the Academy of Television Arts and Sciences in 1985 and has written several books. He lives in New York City with his wife of 63 years.